*A Journey to
Self-Discovery
and Growth
Toward Oneness
in Truth*

ONENESS IN TRUTH WITHOUT END

SASHA-MARIE MARSHALL

*A Journey to
Self-Discovery
and Growth
Toward Oneness
in Truth*

ONENESS IN TRUTH WITHOUT END

SASHA-MARIE MARSHALL

ONENESS IN TRUTH WITHOUT END

A Journey to Self-Discovery and Growth
Toward Oneness in Truth

SASHA-MARIE MARSHALL

Copyright © 2025 Sasha-Marie Marshall

All rights reserved. No part of this book may be reproduced, distributed, stored in a retrieval system, or transmitted in any form or by any means electronic, mechanical, or without the prior written permission from the publisher, except in the case of brief quotations embodied in reviews and certain other noncommercial uses permitted by copyright law.

Published by:

Sasha-Marie Marshall

Austin, TX, United States of America

First Edition: 2025

ISBN: 979-8-9875217-5-5 (hardcover)

ISBN: 979-8-9875217-4-8 (paperback)

ISBN: 979-8-9875217-9-3 (ebook)

Disclaimer:

This book is a work of nonfiction. The information provided is for educational and informational purposes only and should not be considered professional advice. The author and publisher disclaim all liability for any outcomes resulting from the use of this book.

Unless otherwise indicated, Scripture quotations are from

The Halleluyah Scriptures ©2017 (7th edition)

Credits:

Written by: Sasha-Marie Marshall

Book Cover by: Katarina Naskovski

Dedication to Legal Compliance:

Any references to real people, organizations, or events are purely coincidental unless explicitly stated.

*To Yahuah, my Father, belong blessings, honor, glory and power
eon upon eon.*

For the family of Oneness in Truth

*World Without End
So it is. So be it. So let it be.*

INTRODUCTION

"There is no fear in love, but perfect love casts out fear." 1 John 4:18a

Dear Reader,

This book was born out of supernatural experiences with the Spirit of Truth and the events that followed. Even though I came from a Christian background and was baptized in my teenage years, it wasn't until after many such experiences that I was truly delivered from the false systems and beliefs of this world. After several encounters, the proverbial veil was lifted, and I was given the gift to see and experience the spiritual realm while awake in the "physical" body. In real time I could perceive the motives, intentions and spirits of those around me.

These poems are messages the Holy Spirit, the Spirit of Truth, gave me to share with those who would read this book. They were written over the scope of a year and were shared daily on my website: sashamariemarshall.com. The section titles form a poem in and of themselves, a poem about redemption and atonement through Yeshuah Ha'Mashiach, Jesus Christ. As a reader myself, I am always eager to perceive the layers of truth I glean when returning to the words revealed in this book. I take no credit for them, because they belong to the Most High, the One who gave them to me. He spoke and continues to speak from the Kingdom of Heaven within.

My prayer and hope is that as you read and reflect throughout each section of this book, you will come away with deeper discernment and a closer, more intimate walk with the Spirit of Truth in the name of Yeshua Jesus, the Word of Truth.

Much love and eternal blessings to those who read, to those who love and cling to the Spirit of Truth.

Thanks and praises be to the One, true and living Elohim, my Abba forever, Yahuah Most High.

Oneness in Truth Without End
(section titles in lines of four)

Sections I - IV: The Entrance of Light

> *When Comes the Light*
> *Truth Masters Darkness*
> *In the Day and in the Night*
> *Uprooting Unconsciousness*

Sections V - VIII: Light Wars Against Darkness

> *The Word of Life*
> *Piercing Through the Veil*
> *Ended the Strife*
> *Oppressors Weep and Wail*

Sections IX - XII: Light Wins

> *The Lion and the Lamb*
> *Setting Captives Free*
> *No Longer Condemned*
> *A Glorious Victory*

TABLE OF CONTENTS

WHEN COMES THE LIGHT

What Will You Do?	5
Fallen Cedar	7
Exiled	10
The System Is Rigged	12
"Owners" Not Originators	14
Orchestrated	16
Wars, Wars, Everywhere	20
They Love Death, You Love Life	21
Fishers n' Fish Bait	22
Murder Capital Found in Burial	23
Black Hole Entities	24
Lying Lips	25
The Waste Places	26
Kundalini Rising to Hell	27
Slithering, Fading	29
Triangle Inverted, Triangle, Hexagon	30
Truth	31
Conquered Counterfeits	32
Now Resurrected!	33
Truth Remains, Lies Pass Away	34
L.O.V.E.	35
The Kingdom Is Inside o' You	36
True Intentions	38
The Higher Mind, the Sovereign Within	39
Yahuah	41
The Conduit	42
Abassadors	43
Rising to Life	44

TRUTH MASTERS DARKNESS

Unraveling	49
Mindwaves	51
The Mind in You	53

The Unstable Mind	55
The Reprobate Mind	57
Chosen Chaos	59
Masked Mind	61
The Mind of Folly	63
Lifted the Veil	65
Keys	67
Authenticity	69
Reflections	71
Paramount Perceptions	73
Until Full Deliverance	75
The Seasons Within	77
Sudden Shift	79
No Other Voice	81
The Mind Anointed	83
The Journey Within	85
The External Wave	87
Peace in Flow	89
A Thing Called "Beauty"	91
Like Sifted, Shifting Sands	93
To Love an Enemy I	95
To Love an Enemy II	97
Soundness of Mind	99
Lovers in Light	101
Guard Yourself	103
Love Letter to the Truth	105

IN THE DAY AND IN THE NIGHT

Evening	111
Morning	112
Chaos	113
Peace	114
Night	115
Day	116
Darkness	117
Light	118
Pride	119
Purpose	120
Hell	121

Heaven	122
Without	123
Within	124
Illusion	125
Reality	126
Down	127
Up	128
Falsehood	129
Truth	130
Destruction	131
Creation	132
Autumn's Winter	133
Spring's Summer	134
Below	135
Above	136
Waste Place	137
Fruitful Field	138
Desert	139
Living Spring	140
Oneness	141

UPROOTING UNCONSCIOUSNESS

Uprooting	147
A Quickening	148
Pompous Futility	149
Let Them Alone	150
Key Called Humility	151
Desolate Houses	152
Those of the Void	153
No Control	154
Shark-Infested Waters	155
Practicing Lawlessness	156
Dysfunction and Delirium	157
Scripted Life	158
Soul Fruits	159
The Way of Pride	160
Androids of Chaos	161
Wisdom's Daughters	162
Entrapment	163

Light Esteemed!	164
Mind, Will, Emotions	165
Spirit of Truth	166
Trust	167
Subconscious Journey	168
Tree of Life	169
Tree of Good and Evil	170
Deep Waves	171
Radical Acceptance	172
Draconian Cronies	173
Defeated in Discovery	174
Subconscious Healed	175
Total Renewal	176

THE WORD OF LIFE

Kadosh Name	181
Still, Small Voice	182
Highest Frequency	183
Another World	184
Mind Within	185
Well-Lit Lamp	186
Truth Is Light	187
Personhood	188
Truth-Light to Visible Light	189
Word of Elohim	190
Exposed Darkness	191
Sovereign's Control	192
Conquered Fear	193
Occupies the Altar	194
Indwelling	195
Above the Grid	197
In the Heavenlies	198
Shifted the Paradigm	199
True Intimacy	200
Transcendence	201
Eternally Guided	202
Kadosh Council	203
Vision	204
Purposeful Partners	205

No Looking Back	206
Metamorphosis	207
Onward, Upward	208
DNA Inscribed	209
Scroll	210
Book of Life	211
World Without End	212

PIERCING THROUGH THE VEIL

What Do You Seek?	217
What You Seek, Seeks You	218
Who Are You?	219
You Are Who You Are	220
Who Sees You?	221
You See You	222
Who Knows You?	223
Remember Who You Are	224
Where Are You?	225
You Are Now?	226
Where Do You Come From?	227
From the Realms Unseen	228
Why Are You Here?	229
Meaning, Purpose	230
What Is Meaning?	231
What Is Purpose?	232
Where Are You Going?	233
Positioning	234
What Do You Hear?	235
Frequency of Sound, of Light	236
What Is Ignorance?	237
Blindness	238
What Is Death?	239
Extremely Low Consciousness	240
What Is Life?	241
Spirit of Truth	242
What Is Fear?	243
Egocentric Mind	244
What Is Freedom?	245
Truth and Light	246

ENDED THE STRIFE

Riddance to Welcome	251
A Voice in This Place	252
Peace	253
Absence, Presence	254
Create More than Consume	255
Sustenance	256
True Reality	257
One With Truth	258
Accord	259
Self-Mastery	260
Authentic Authority	261
Fulfillment	262
Allegiance	263
Established	264
Confidence	265
A Higher Plane	267
Mind-Worlds	268
Eyes	269
Four Faces	270
Eagle	271
Adam	272
Lion	273
Cherub	274
Wings	275
Right Hand	276
Feet	277
"Oh, Wheel"	278
Firmament	279
Service	280
Realm-to-Realm	281
From Above	282

OPPRESSORS WEEP AND WAIL

Gnashing of Teeth	287
A Chosen Death	288
Cyclical Sea	289
Dark Alignment	290
City's Enemies Defeated	291

Decoys of the Night	292
Alive but Dead	293
Illusions of Separation	294
Vortices of Chaos	295
The Technology of Flesh	296
Balancing the Up and Down	297
Upside-Down World	298
Targeting the World Above	299
The Tares	300
The Goats	301
By Their Fruit	302
Their Roots	303
Spiritual Laziness	304
Vain Form	305
Idols	306
Hell Raiser	307
Wicked Prize	308
Mortal Immortals	309
Creatures from Beneath	310
Privileged Destruction	311
Attack of the Trolls	312
Crooked, Twisted Serpent	313
Wild by Nature	314
Distorted and Disturbed	315
Taken in Tyranny	316
Wicked Tango	317

THE LION AND THE LAMB

A Teaching, a Learning	323
In the Beginning	324
The Word	325
In the Garden	326
The Lamb Within	327
No Greater Love	328
Christ in Me	329
Garment of Light	330
Sacrifice, What Is?	331
Truth's Blood	332
The Door	333

The Bellwether	334
L.O.V.E. Requires Spirit	335
A Quickening Flow	336
Our Goshen	337
The Lamb	338
Shout of the King	339
Identity	340
Never Alone	341
In Guarding I	342
Seed in Yahuah	343
Tribe	344
Solitude	345
Rest	346
Well Fed	347
Almighty	348
Forever Favored	349
Looking Up	350
At the Ending	351
All Authority	352

SETTING CAPTIVES FREE

Born and Shaped	357
A House Robbed	358
Falsehood Is a World	359
Truth Is a Kingdom	360
Better to Be than to Feel	361
Feelings a Fleeting	362
Not the Same	363
Decoy No Longer	364
Emotions	365
Being	366
Within the Soul	367
Internal Invincible Army	368
Breaking Bondage	369
Deceptive Dominion	370
Trauma Prince	371
On Wings of Deliverance	372
Prince of Peace	373
Truth, Love, Justice	374

They Say Truth Hurts	375
Our Rock	376
A House Built	377
Hiccup	378
Why Pain?	379
Purpose Is Power	380
Messengers Multiplied	381
Light	382
Pain, Purpose, Power	383
A Sure Word	384
Enemies Expelled	385
The Great Calm	386
Captives Made Free	387

NO LONGER CONDEMNED

New Creature	393
Eternity Now	394
The Crossings	395
Not Condemned	396
Autonomy	397
Perception	398
A New World	399
Mindset Is Vital	400
Pricked Pride	401
The Miracle of Tears	402
A Triggering	403
Balm for the Soul	404
Crown "Jewels"	405
Houses: From Sand to Rock	406
Converted	407
Held Fast	408
Fortified City	409
From Web to Way	411
Breakthrough	412
Courage	413
Revealed	414
Resistance	415
Emanations	416
One Voice	417

Eternal Family	418
Ripples	419
Watch and Pray (Jamaican Patois)	420

A GLORIOUS VICTORY

Life Eternal	425
True Power	426
The Lamb's Wife	427
Heel of Power	428
Bygones	430
Sons of Light	431
A Place Called Peace	432
Serenity	433
Love-Kissed	434
Reign Eternal	435
Consuming Fire	436
Fine Brass	437
White Linen	438
Eye Salve	439
Crowns	440
Living Crystal	441
Sapphire Stone	442
Throne Room	443
Foundation	444
Living Stones	445
Kingdom	446
An Appointed Time	447
Crescendo	448
Full Throttle	449
The Fulness of Victory	450
An Eternal Rejoicing	451
Family of One	452
So Be It, So Let It Be	453
Acknowledgments	455
About the Author	457

WHEN COMES THE

WHAT WILL YOU DO?

What will you do?
When you've gained
All the world and lost you
When you have the car,
The house, the family, too
What more will you want?
Will you be satisfied?
Riding the high, gratified?
With feelings of euphoria
Your idea of liberty
What will you do?

Tell me what you'll do
When you've gained it all and lost you
When you've achieved the fame
When they all know your name
Tell me is it worth it
The momentary pleasure
Was it all that much better
Than peace?
Tell me what you'll do

Yah gives me Himself
He satisfies me completely
And I wondered what I'd do
If it were me, would my desires
Like yours soon expire
Only to be replaced by another?
No, I've already found
Peace
Yah gives me Himself

What will you do?
What else will you want?
Why?

What *more* do you want?
Why?
Why do you want these things?
Why?
Why do you seek the things that can't satisfy?
What will you do?

It is your choice
In which you'll rejoice
One day though, I hope you'll
Seek Truth and
Know in the end
Nothing outside is more
Valuable to explore
Than the
You
Within
It is your choice

FALLEN CEDAR

The fallen cedar was in the heights of the trees
Was also found among the ships of the seas
The cherub among the living stones of eden
He was the self same serpent in the garden

Cosmic dust the living stones did create
Yah blew the breath of life, living souls did make
They lived among the trees of paradise
There the cedar envied them with green eyes

He didn't much enjoy the serving
The servant wanted them worshiping
Iniquity was found within his cruel plan
To kill them with shortening their lifespan

The fruit of his temptation was sensual
Fornication and a flesh suit his main goal
Fell one, fell two, carnal mind installed
Found themselves trapped no *wear* with all

The Voice of Yah found them in this whirlwind
His grace and mercy clothed them with coats of skin
The serpent now the ruler in his stead
Adam walked in shame, lowered head

Took his wife when driven into the realm of earth
Twins, one serpent and one man, did she birth
The offspring of the serpent killed the younger
Cain marked as beast, welcomed no longer

There began the struggle, the hostility
Humanity none the wiser to this treachery
The cedar in rebellion against the Most High
His foolish pride and selfishness, the reasons why

Over centuries still had access to the heavens
He tempted the princes of the other realms
Fell three, fell six, their nations ravaged
No idea that their rulers were savages

They worshiped birds, beasts, and nature
Their princes guiding them to this structure
Rebellion now widespread in the earth realm
The fallen trees of the garden at the helm

Mixed and mingled with creatures and mankind
The earth was filled with violence, corrupt, unkind
Adamic, the only line without serpent blood
Yah made a plan in order to keep some good

Destroyed by flood to save man alive
Restarted so humanity could survive
But as soon as those souls got off the boat
The fallen ones were already at their throat

The whole world was soon back in darkness
The cedar and friends bent on chaos, mess
Finally the Most High sent His Son
Who after warring said, "It is done!"

Even to the death He didn't give up
And now things are about to wrap up
The fallen cedar deciding it wasn't enough
Went to gather other nations in a huff

Confederate, they plot n' scheme to waste man
Already colluding, another lethal plan
Foolish pride won't inherit earth, this they know
But delusion's got them continuing their vain show

An example the fallen will remain
Of pompous chaos, hell, and pain
They were a lesson for all and humanity
With their own allotment content to be

To the All-Wise El, the Most High
The One who heard His people's cry
Be honor, majesty, peace galore
Love be multiplied forevermore!

EXILED

Exiled in the mind down under
Outside, where the wild things grow
Their spirits fractured, ripped apart
Dimmed by ember's glow

The ember needed Spirit-energy
To feed it fuel to burn
The beings exiled used for this
They soon would have to learn

Various beings walked the realm
At first it sounded crazy
But they would soon experience
The parasitic and the lazy

The egotistic ember
With serpentine smile
Wanted creatures to worship him
Like a spoiled, ill-tempered child

To be the center of attention
The glory a frenzied drug
No kindness shown to deserve it
Yet still their worship wrung

Vain deceit and falsehood
His lengthy tail did spin
Fervent seeking for the Truth
Their only way to win

This Truth was the spoken Word
That came from the Most High
Their weapon of warfare was the tongue
Speaking Truth with a loud cry

Soon to be exiled no more
Their renewed state of mind
The Knowing to which they clung
Bringing to the Land Divine

THE SYSTEM IS RIGGED

Watch out for the easy,
The opportunistic, and the lame
Devils sent to use n' abuse you
Just for pocket change
Stolen power for making
Unjust gain
And for what? The admiring eyes
Of all the people round about
To say they're human and exist
Around the lot

It's because inside they're
Just an empty shell
The real them no longer there
So the demon must be fed
Masquerades like one of us just to get by
So it can feast on the
Innocent without a prying eye
Rebuke them the whole lot
Send them to the pit from which they came
Give others a fighting chance to not
Be victim to their game

They're here to drag other souls
Into the pit in which they dwell
So get on the path and
Get rid of them quick
Be aware and understand what a narcissist is
It's a label given to the devil and his kids
A solid foundation of the Truth
Will keep you from destruction
But that doesn't mean you can't fall prey
To the enemy's machinations
Be sober n' be vigilant
They're vipers

When we fell into the flesh
It was game on for the brutes
The whole time all your life
Spawning Beelzebubs after you
Body jumping from husk to husk
Trying to destroy the Truth
Of who you are, why you're here
N' trying to get rid of you
It's like the plane that crashed
On that island in "Lost"
Except you're the plane in the system
And the enemy is the host
A beast of illusions and delusions of the mind
Don't sleep or fall for it
'Cause you'll end up in a bind
Sad, depressed, and paying for it in the end
The system is rigged, it's a rigged system
Understand that now and you'll
Save yourself from many sorrows

"OWNERS" NOT ORIGINATORS

It's the sequence of Life
What's this Fibonacci game?
Every design has a designer
Give the Creator His praise
They brand cars, clothes n' everything
Give Him the glory due His name
By Him they even live, move,
And have the ability to breathe
The audacity to curse
The One Whom they bereave
How can they claim
The bang had no Banger?
Let's see them build a house
Without lifting a finger
Or construct anything, no engineers
And architects working together
Tired of this disrespectful rebellion
The enemy roaring like a Lion
Going around seeking whom
He may devour
His seed stealing the praise
Of the Heavenly Father
Copied styles, stolen history,
And lies aplenty
Carved their faces everywhere
To "show" they "own" many
"Owners" not originators of anything
The Tom-foolery coming to end
As we sing
Is fallen Babylon
Babylon is fallen
For making merchandise,
Merchandising souls of men
For lying, stealing,
And killing too

Finally your end
Has come unto you
Babylon is fallen
Is fallen Babylon
And they shall not be found
Anymore
At
All

ORCHESTRATED

Act I - Inception

Where are the costumes?
I don't know, beats me
Action, on the count of 1, 2, 3
But I wasn't ready
Neither were any of us
They're ready, let's not make a fuss

Look at the camera
Come on, give us a smile
Yeah, that's it, perfected the meek n' mild
But they're neither
And they've known it since birth
However, only the meek shall inherit the earth

Do you think it fair?
It matters not my thoughts
Only the actions that in this life I wrought
Were you successful?
With the pretending, I mean
Maybe, the director seemed pleased with my scene

Act II - Awareness

Cut! Hey, what was that?
Promise, I did the best I could
Well, this line of business leave you should
How do you do it so well?
All that make belief
Getting out was such a relief

They let her go
I guess she couldn't hang
No, just wouldn't put up with the shebang

Why do you?
What do you mean? Such is life
Well, I'd rather have peace than all that strife

Peace? That sounds boring
Does it really though?
I'd rather be bored than a vain show
Come back to set
Maybe, he'll let you reprise your role
No way, that life my peace stole

Act III - Decision

Look who it is
Hey, long time no see
That's been perfectly fine by me
How're things going with you?
Took my life back down from a dusty shelf
Where I'd left it, best I could've done for myself

You still in that line of work?
You know, I mean the acting
Still spending your life make pretending?
And if we are, what is it to you?
No need to get defensive
A question, simply to make you pensive

To be honest,
We want out, but it's too late
Like penguins that did already mate
It's a pact we've made
And it's until the end
Our director, a tyrant, will not bend

Act IV - Realization

The islands were not found
The mountains fled away

The Great White Throne on Judgement Day
Whoa! This set looks so real
Advanced green screen
The lights, bright, serene

Hey, shh, be quiet
I don't think this is an act
We're suspended on nothing, that is a fact
Don't look up
It's a scary Summit
Not down either, an even scarier plummet

Do you know who He Is?
The One seated on the throne
Remember that girl? He's the Almighty One she'd shone
So that was real?
Seriously, you still have to ask?
You can't tell, no part of this is a mask?

Act V - Truth

This isn't fair
I mean, who knew You existed?
My whole life the Truth they twisted
Our decision?
Yes, it was our choice to make
But spare us, please, for Your Name's sake

To the New Earth?
Yeah, of course, why not?
It's better than with death to be caught
"Peace sounds boring,"
Is that not so?
Why to a "boring" place would you want to go?

Hey, we could liven it up
It doesn't have to be that way
A little drama add every other day

Off with them!
And the saying remains true
Good and evil mixed, cannot be the two

WARS, WARS, EVERYWHERE

Star Wars
Stone Wars
Power-of-the-tongue Wars
Energy Wars
Spirit Wars
Life and Death Wars

This is Spiritual Warfare
Fight the good fight, never despair
This world, wicked, lies n' devils filled
But the Truth in us, soon revealed
When? You ask, the time is now
The blink of an eye will show you how

Wake up in glory
The Esteem of Yah see
Oneness in Truth is our portion
Meanwhile for them, total consumption
They chose *it*, not us, their selfish *pride*
Colluded together, saying die or ride

Realms split, north-south magnet
Marvel no more, you *chose* it
Living stones, Up
Infinity stones, Down
Forever to sup
The others, lost crown

Star Wars
Stone Wars
Power-of-the-tongue Wars
Energy Wars
Spirit Wars
Life and Death Wars

THEY LOVE DEATH, YOU LOVE LIFE

They love death, they've admitted
They love death, *you* don't fool with it
They love death, they've admitted
They love death, *you* don't fool with it

They wish to know you, but you don't do carnality
Wish things to last, then they gotta live spiritually
The flesh is corrupted, can't inherit eternity
Carnal mind is temporal, to perish utterly

Every opportunity they had to choose kindness
Allowed their inflated ego the helm to them debase
Showing that they instead love and practice wickedness
The earth and its inhabitants witness to this case

Like a ghoul and ghost, their body a phantom of its host
An abandoned home of the soul that is lost
Wandering unencumbered from coast to coast
They're haunted, unfettered by the heat and the frost

With violence they threw Truth to the ground
To mischievous madness is despotic ruin
'Cause of their own actions, they're no longer found
To the womb and the wound of the grave they go in

Showing Himself that He's the One with whom to reckon
Truth Himself resurrected, at the right hand of the Father
Kiss the Son lest He be angry, the last day beckon
His holy angels in the earth, His people gather

You love Life, you're chosen
You love Life, *they* can't fool with Him
You love Life, you're chosen
You love Life, *they* can't fool with Him

FISHERS N' FISH BAIT

Fish bait, one and all
Fish bait, fish bait, while they fall

For vanities, powers, souls so reckless
They were sell-fish and not selfless
Offered up their own family as fish bait
Forever young? No, forever dying, too late

They were a serpent-eat-serpent kind of race
Cain-Abel-ing each another, hiding their face
Given another chance, they'd do it again
Cheering all about it on their we*a*k-en'

There was, by contrast, the Adamic line
Drawn by Dragon's tail from the Mind Divine
Hurled to the earth, they suffered sore
But their Father had a plan in store

His Word said, "I will make you fishers of men"
His Way to win souls back to HEA-*ven*[1]
He came to reveal Yah's Truth of One
Forever victorious are we in the Son

Fishers, never fish bait
Fishers, fishers, on Yah we wait

---

1. HEA - Happily Ever After

MURDER CAPITAL FOUND IN BURIAL

They called it *murder* capital where they murdered for capital
Didn't know they'd be the ones to be found in the burial
Created a beast system and got themselves locked in it
Now trappers are trapped, and chasers chased, sad innit?

Flipped the world right side up, glad things have changed
Their lies transmuted to Truth, now look who's deranged
Thought they'd be the head, but instead became tailed
Now the mockers are mocked, and the liars all failed

BLACK HOLE ENTITIES

The vampires, the ghouls, and the parasites
Don't just exist in Hollywood fantasies and websites
Put the energies around you to the test
Discernment will help you realize they're not the best

Friends, parents, or partners, I don't care
If they have no intrinsic Light of life, the pit they share
Refrain from getting tangled in their outward look
Their carnal flesh and expressions your heart mistook

It doesn't pay to be naive, you should know
Inwardly they froth and fume for your inner glow
Would you approach a whirlwind or a tornado?
Tantamount to getting caught up with them, oh no!

The question here is do you really L.O.V.E. yourself?
Then, you wouldn't allow another to harm your health
Their mask on the several times they've been good to you
Doesn't any inner, soul-searching goodness prove

Black holes, vortices leading to the abyss
Staying connected with them, your life's goodbye kiss
I know, it's sad, but mourn their death today
They've made a choice, now make yours, go or stay

---

1. L.O.V.E. - Living in Oneness Vs. Ego

LYING LIPS

They **say** they love
When hate is what they **do**
Don't cling to empty words
That lying lips issue
Actions over sentiments
Energy won't lie to you

Throat an open grave
Deceit rising out
Mischievous madness
That's what they spout
People pleasers, attention seekers
Many of them chasing clout

In this world of opposites
They say, "Be kind," when they're not it
False masks on at every hour
Fooling many, blind to their skit
Being nice *is* their cover
Inside won't change, no, not one bit

When you stand within the Truth
None of this can get past you
Falsehood buried in their tongue
Killing them, 'cause you withdrew
Found no longer by those cheats,
Manipulators, and abusers too

THE WASTE PLACES

Falsehood is a waste place
Lies are its matter, fecal
They mess and find pleasure
Diabolical, devilish, lethal

Finding it impossible to choose the right,
Scavenging the dead, a devil, Tasmanian
Always seeking to destroy those who're alive,
Watching to catch prey, a dog, Siberian

Pride is a waste place
The inflated ego is its matter, chaotic
Wars, wars, and rumors of wars,
Murdering many and calling it patriotic

Finding it impossible to truly love others,
Manipulating craftily, a serpent, Red Dragon
Always seeking to funnel live bait into their web,
Biting cyclically, a Sydney spider, Australian

Lust is a waste place
Unbridled appetite is its matter, impulsive
They seek to fulfill their constant cravings,
Uncontrolled actions to that end, compulsive

Finding it impossible to see others
As more than just an object, just a creature, nonhuman
Always wandering about, an empty shell,
Feening for the next high, an addict, *sub*human

KUNDALINI RISING TO HELL

Wide Gate, Broad Way

It may seem ***sssss*** weet, but the enemy always counterfeits
All while secretly offering his victims diabolical treats
Telling humanity to ground, to ***sssss*** it down
To raise their own vibration to the crown,
The attempt to climb up some other way
To reap the benefits without the pay
But can they handle the sorrow
That comes with the "*borrow*"
The thief, and the robbery
Results of the treachery?
All of it *stolen* energy
Death a final synergy
They have no clue
What it is they do
Rising to the pit
While they sit
Falling fodder
To the worm
In the gutter
Of the
Abyss
Below

"'Stolen waters are sweet, and bread in secret is pleasant.' But he does not know that the dead are there, her guests are ***in the depths of the grave***." Proverbs 9:17-18 (*emphasis added* - **realm of the dead**)

Following one's own way or a voice other than that of the Word of Truth will not lead to a good end. Truth, Structure, Order — these are vital in finding the Way to Life. Finally, a great many who have sought after the kundalini and similar practices have ended up in fear and pain, with anxiety, depression, hallucinations, etc. It is not a practice that leads to Life. It is yet another strong man, a lure, a trap for unassuming souls set by the darkness of this world.

"Let all be done decently and in order." 1 Corinthians 14:40

"The berakah [blessings] of Yahuah makes one rich, and He adds no pain with it." Proverbs 10:22

[1]Kundalini

---

1. *Kundalini Etymology* (Sanskrit)
   Kund — "pit, cave, or deep place"
   Lini — "to be absorbed in energy"
   Ini can be translated as "power"
   Kundalin — "serpent"

SLITHERING, FADING

Slithering,
Slithering and withering,
Think themselves triumphant in it, shivering
With glee

Mirroring,
Mirroring and reflecting,
Their actions onto themselves projecting
Slipping right into their own snare

Writhing,
Writhing and sliding,
The agony coming after their deriding
Of the innocent one

Falling,
Falling and bawling,
Their words an unrepentant drawling
To avoid consequences

Fading,
Fading and evading,
Escapism, their whole lives masquerading
'Til they're ... no more

TRIANGLE INVERTED, TRIANGLE, HEXAGON

The triple 6 of Revelation isn't what it seems
It's the banking system in the 7 streams
6 sides, 6 triangles, and 6 vertices[1]
Their wealth, trading, merchandise in the 7 seas

Called it war against "weapons of mass destruction"
While they built their beast system, mass *corruption*
The seas? Peoples, tongues and nations
A set up, blinding true revelations

It's a trap, the world system around you
To lure you to the pit they've all gone to
If you really think on it, it's plain to see
The gross lack of justice, the insanity

They venerate the carnal mind just like before
The ancient world destroyed by the very same lore
Stop waiting for a mark, the world's already in
They keep baiting n' switching, while you sleep again

That triangular symbol over their eyes
To institute their mind, their system of lies
If you buy into it, fully converted
Stuck upside down, wicked

Overcoming the mark, conversion to life again
One with the Kingdom of the world within
The heavenly host also cheering you on
Fight that fight, He's already won!

---

1. King David never created a star for himself. Research the origin of the star which is falsely called the "Star of David" and you will find out the truth. There is no basis for such a star in the Word.

TRUTH

"Buy the Truth and sell it not"
If delusion's all you've got
Stick to the lies and you will rot
From the inside, come to naught

Hate the Truth and you will see
Just how fake your life will be
Stuck a fool within the sea
Cyclical grave for eternity

Don't like me and I'm fine with that
Made Truth my home, salvation hat
All liars move just like a rat
Words of Life will make 'em flat

This is warfare without the guns
Liars wield their unruly tongues
With the Truth we make 'em run
Back to the pit from which they come

Truth reigns supreme after it all
Falsehood got their final fall
Never returned from behind the wall
Of the gulf fixed between the hull

CONQUERED COUNTERFEITS

In the upside-down world, they replaced Truth
With delusion, deceit and lying vanity
Clarity they turned into vague obscurity
Enabled dysfunction by calling it compassion
And exchanged integrity for niceness,
Foresight for manipulation n' darkness

Venerating anything but Truth's supremacy
Their falsehood, an atrocity, unmitigated audacity
They forsook reliability for unstable felicity
True Love they swapped out for jealousy,
Codependence, selfishness and lust
Instead of embracing the Father's Way, True n' Just

In the World without end, the World within
Truth stood firm, warring, never giving up the fight
All counterfeits of the night He put to flight
The enemy howled and barked, angered as the Prince
Rescued His sheep's mind from their prison,
Setting captives free, n' look, they've risen!

With scales removed from their eye
They speak Truth to life and to power
Renewed, restored, persevering to the last hour
Withstanding all the fakes with the Words of Life
They remembered who they are, *Whose* they are
Guarded by Truth-Light n' ready for war

NOW RESURRECTED!

The lying wonders of the principalities,
Created the carnal mind, their realities
Rebelled against the Father's Truth and Love,
Resulting in their exile from the Realm above

Cast into the darkness down below
They invented lies, their vain show
Made themselves flesh bodies in which to dwell
Several realms, existence in their own hell

Tempted their former brethren from heaven
Brought them to the place they'd leavened
The war was on, the Truth against the lies
And the Heavenly Father heard their cries

Yah Sent His Word of Truth to dispel their myth
Their selfish minds, falsehoods to wrestle with
Mashiach won the war, paying with His own blood
Word of Yah living *in* us, now *wrestle* we could

We'd slept in the lies, in the dust of the earth
But through His Holy Spirit new creatures birth
Chosen, we stand for the Spirit of Truth
The Word of Yah the Father our only Booth

We've turned flipped right side up, no longer down
"Hold fast what you have so no one take your crown"
That's the command we received from the Word
Take care to heed, guard, and do what you heard

The Truth has given us life, we're resurrected
HalleluYah, thank you Yeshuah, our Prince it did!
Laying down His life so we could live again
Reconciled us to the Father, World without end!

TRUTH REMAINS, LIES PASS AWAY

Truth will remain, will remain
Lies will pass away, pass away

Lies and fears, fears and lies
Whole system seen through renewed eyes,
The *now* is when you'll realize
The stupid game and its stupid prize

A higher plane for a higher mind
If this you seek, then you shall find
The darkness will grow more unkind
'Cause when up high, you they can't bind

In high places, tongue taught for battle
Thousands against, you they can't rattle
The war is on, now get in the saddle
Word of Truth in you, they can't addle

The Word spoken from the tongue
Is the victory from which you wrung
The confidence their falsehood stung
Falling to the pit above which they hung

Lies pass away, pass away
Truth remains, remains

L.O.V.E.

Light from Powers of the realms above
Dispelling every ounce of darkness
Can't take credit for this Word
It's all Yah and His greatness

Truth resurrected so that I might live
Forever, and ever, and ever still
Ego dies daily so that in Truth I do
Not my own but my Father's will

How deep does this go?
To the other side of creation
Where the root of all things grow
Above, obedience; below, insubordination

To make no more mistakes
Lured by this world's desire
The Word to perfect me
Making me Yah's treasure

A city set upon a hill
Light penetrating the night
A sheep dedicated to His Way
Loving all and putting a thousand to flight

---

1. L.O.V.E. - Living in Oneness Vs. Ego

THE KINGDOM IS INSIDE O' YOU

They don't get it
They never do
The Kingdom is inside o' you
They don't get it
They never do
The Kingdom is inside o' you

Why do they keep telling
On the pulpits selling
The lies about heaven's location
The Word Himself said
In countless scriptures read
The importance of the heart's invocation

It's not about looking in the sky
As the actual Truth passes by
Regarding the state of the heart, mind, and soul
Without a transformed mind
The Kingdom they'll never find
If anything outside beckons the goal

Go into the secret place
That's where you'll find the trace
Of the Most High's still small voice
Be still and know
Then to you He'll show
His Kingdom without all that outside noise

Too many friends in the throng
Make the journey oh so long
If only you could get by yourself
Turn off the radio waves
Moments of solitude to crave
Allow the True Light enter you Himself

For the Word to remain fresh
You have to crucify the flesh
Eschewing anyone or anything that it venerates
From the programmed ego to depart
With a broken and a contrite heart
The life of His Son through you He'll generate

But if you have heaped up teachers
Those many diabolical preachers
Who the Word says care nothing for the sheep
To be dependent on them
The real Truth unlikely to stem
Then, sadly you'll forever sleep

They don't get it
They never do
The Kingdom is inside o' you
They don't get it
They never do
The Kingdom is inside o' you

Within you is a portal. However for eternal life in knowing the Father, there is only One Key to that portal. That Key ... is the Word of Yahuah, Who is the Way, the Truth, and the Life.

> "And having been asked by the Pharisees when the reign of Elohim would come, He answered them and said, 'The reign of Elohim does not come with intent watching, nor shall they say, 'Look here!' or 'Look there!' For look, the reign of Elohim is in your midst!'" Luke 17:20-21

> "I am the door. Whoever enters through Me, he shall be saved, and shall go in and shall go out and find pasture. The thief does not come except to steal, and to slaughter, and to destroy. I have come that they might possess hai [life], and that they might possess it beyond measure." John 10:9-10

TRUE INTENTIONS

True intentions of the heart
Resolution, vision and clarity
Under the guidance of Yahuah
Eagle-eyed, a sharpened reality

In the world within, the one of the spirit
Nothing can escape from the Truth
Thoughts and intentions of the heart
Ensnared the prideful who tried using you
Not foreseeing the results of their own actions
Their mind reels, shocked and confused
It never occurred that there could be
One apt and alert to their ruse
Nothing absconds from Oneness in Truth
Serpentine ways will always lose

THE HIGHER MIND, THE SOVEREIGN WITHIN

From the Higher Mind creating,
From the planes above shaping
The realm
Below

Flowing, illuminating, empowering
Source Energy to our energy, moving
The host in
The plane
Below

From the Sovereign within forming,
From the world inside manifesting
The life
Without

Transforming, healing, renewing
Holy Spirit to our spirit, restoring
The representative in
The world
Without

YAHUAH

I
Am
Because
Yah, You Are
Love transcendent
For all eternity resplendent
No worldly gimmick, nor ploy
In Your Presence is the fullness of joy
Grateful am I to have been found by You,
Lost as I was in falsehood, down, feeling blue
When Your Breath of Truth entered, filling my lungs
Your Words of Life scattering thousands of lying tongues
Placing me to stand firmly on hinds feet like those of a deer
Your Holy Spirit guiding me, teaching me, making the Way clear
You set me on Your Holy Mountain, Zion, my City, my Home forevermore
No one can ever compare to Who You Are, how You heal, how You restore
"Blessing, honor, glory and power be to Him Who sits on the throne, and to the Lamb for ever and ever!" So be it. So let it be. HalleuYah! Praise Yah!

THE CONDUIT

The oracle, the conduit
Of the heavenly flow
Cerebrospinal fluid infused
Yah's magnificent glow
Electromagnetic current
Entering through the gates
Lifting up their heads
On Abba we wait

The Word of Yah
Truth inscribed in our DNA
Our inward parts
Witness to His wonderful Name
Not unto us, not unto us
Oh, Abba Yah
Unto Your Name alone
Pertains la gloria!

HalleluYahuah!
Praise Yah!

AMBASSADORS

Empowered by the Father
Mouthpiece for no other
The Lion and the Lamb mentality
Kindness to the kind
Pure to the divine
Twisted to the wicked, judging energy

Humility the key
Pride the tomfoolery
The one filled with it will be no more
For they choose their own way
In dysfunction to stay
Our enemy, in death, sour, sore

Empathy to those who need a bit
Little to those who lack it
We respond to the call of duty
By Wisdom we perceive
The soul yearning to receive
A Word, an act from Truth's serenity

Through the places we enter,
Causing His enemies to scatter
Their backs turned, heading some other way
But those who draw near
His Holy Spirit endears
Preparing them to rise in this Last Day

RISING TO LIFE

Life in this world, a series of lessons
The Anointed said difficult is the Way
This world a downgraded reality
A lower mind, a darker ray

A need so dire to be fully conscious
Of every thought and its next act
Be aware in the *now* moment
A sound mind to remain intact

Knowledge of the Eternal
Oneness in Truth, a balm to the soul
With no one else to be compared
No words enough to Yah extol

Rising, seated in heavenly places
To His Word dedication and loyalty
No competitor, no living rival
Falsehood defeated by Truth's Royalty

MASTERS DARKNESS

UNRAVELING

Developed in 3D, in the heart of the earth
Subjected to vanity at the moment of birth

Wrestling with the carnal mind since infancy
Unaware of the traps in the cyclical sea

Lured in by looks, the pride of it all
Fancy outer shells concealing the fall,

The wickedness and rebellion against the Truth,
A world of confusion bent on ensnaring you

Their power lies in falsehood and they love it so
Don't expect a conscience, theirs seared long ago

Decoys as *family* and *friends* around you,
Side eyeing as most of them aren't even true

If they do not follow the Word of Yahuah
There's no Light of Truth in them, no glory halleluyah

They've made themselves a trick of the mind,
Choose Truth and they'll disappear as you bind

All negative energies and foul spirits around
See behind the veil, beyond the sky and the ground

Truth of Yah multiplied from the realm within
Resurrection only to those who've awakened

Wise ones of Yahuah, a restored crown reach
The wicked choose wickedness, falsehood their speech

144 thousand, sealed and ready for victory
Overspreading scourge to abolish their enemy

All had the chance to make a choice
Fallen ones *taken* as the saints rejoice

"Just and true are Your ways, oh King of saints
Who will not revere You and glorify Your Name?"

MINDWAVES

A false reality by false eyes met
What *you* see is what *you* get

Visible light only a part of the spectrum
A limited frequency, a vibration, a hum

Fleshly eyes can only see so much
The electromagnetic range leaving such

Vast footprints to explore
Low or high, the spirits soar

In all hours you must be apt to see
What lies behind the cyclical sea

A limited mind will make it impossible
But with Truth-Light *all* things are possible

Adhering to Truth, with your life guarding
Of a surety you will find it rewarding

To be lifted out of a darkened reality
To explore more than condensed carnality

The higher planes of existence above
Drawn by a heightened, transcendent love

Pureness, wholeness, fullness of joy
No longer a slave, no longer employed

By lower spirits, but standing in the El of Truth
Of peace, and kindness, and goodness too

The mind of flesh could never get you there
To the minds above, to the worlds so fair

An enLightened eternity in peace and bliss
In stark contrast to the pained abyss

Where beings of darkness delight in the torture
Of those souls who chose that departure

THE MIND IN YOU

It's not in the size and space of a place
But in the vital place of your mind space

The mind of this world left untreated
Will leave you down, destitute, depleted

Of spirit-energy and a purpose-driven life
A meaningful existence exchanged for strife

An antagonistic relationship with yourself
Leaving your very soul caged on a shelf

Fragmented, disjointed, moving to-and-fro
Lost, dead, robbed of Light's inner glow

An empty shell of who you once were
"Living the life," yet everything's a blur

Going through the motions, yet feeling none
Wounded and bruised, yet feeling numb

Until Truth on high came down to earth
Your life to revive, affording you rebirth

Spirit and Life are Yah's Words spoken
Keeping you, now healed, no longer broken

The Word said, "Let this mind be in you,
The mind of the Anointed," tried and true

One of humility and obedience
To the Word of Truth, full adherence

No standard of deviation to the left nor right,
Leaving everything behind that took your might,

And your will to do His Word
Now fully loyal, fully assured

The Way of Truth leads to the Father
And to Him comparable is no other

THE UNSTABLE MIND

Altered mind state
Born a blank slate

On a family reliant
With start unpleasant

Trauma to mind and body
Drawn away from nice to naughty

Practicing dysfunction from a tender age
A lethal foundation to set their life's stage

Those around them merely players
Some extras, others main characters

While they hang out in the pit
People pleasing, people, please it

Is a tad bit strange the way
Their thoughts and mind sway

Depending on the given company,
The one trying to be seen by many

Who truly could care less
Distracted by their *own* mess

As the unstable minds reel
Caught up by the emotions they feel

A turbulent whirlwind, round and round
Up and down, confusion bound

Found hot, other times cold
Their night of chaos never grows old

One, two, four, eight, seven, five
One, two, four, eight, seven, five

The unstable mind in the cyclical sea
The Truth will they ever be able to see?

THE REPROBATE MIND

From the spiritual to the carnal mind
The natural man in the flesh to bind

In the fleshly mind, make a reprobate
All they want is to take, take, take

And take some more, never to give
A lack mindset, all elusive

Hateful, full of maliciousness
Envious, all covetousness

Unmerciful, yet desiring mercy
Unstable, yet seeking consistency

Are you gonna tell 'em or shall I?
Living in a fairytale won't justify

Any of their thoughts or their actions
And none of their strange inventions

Since they love what doesn't profit
Let them alone to wallow in it

A sow taking pleasure in a dirty pit
A dog returning to its own vomit

They don't feel sorry, neither should you
Conscience seared to everything true

Surrounding their heart is a callus
Therefore, expect them to be callous

No more humanity, entirely beast
Chaotic, killing after their feast

On an unassuming soul in their net
Malignant, malicious, appetite wet

To destroy the light they managed to find
Nothing as cruel as the reprobate mind

CHOSEN CHAOS

Controlling, wanting to be master,
their actions end up in a disaster

of broken relationships. They try to turn your day
into darkness, your peace into an obscured ray.

The mind that revels in chaos,
mischief, madness and every ruckus,

thrives on making a mess,
creating tension and high stress.

At first you might find it confusing,
the odd behavior and intentional gaslighting.

Beginning to question your own reality,
walking on eggshells to regain some stability,

you grab on to caution and make it your friend.
Changing yourself, you're willing to bend

to regain lost peace. But the chaotic mind wills it
to take first a piece and then another, bit by bit

consuming the life-energy of its prey.
Their goal, their aim, is for you to stay

until you are overcome by their night,
with no more connection to the source of Light

to fight. You think you can change or save them
from their dark world? Their chaos stems

from their own *choice* to serve the creature,
severing their connection to the Father, Creator

of the kingdom of heaven within. They chose
the ego, a self-centeredness that arose

from a depth of desire to be seen as strong,
to be venerated, and held higher than the throng

MASKED MIND

A master mind is the masked mind,
Hiding in plain sight, so others don't find

The creepy crawlies creepy crawlin'
Mask on, pretending, feigned life, all in

The mind of this world, a realm of darkness
Its many deceptions souls' energy harness

For all among us who still do not know,
Evil lurks, using light as its show

Smiling, smizing at the prey they're desiring
Sharks in the water, bloodthirsty, feening

Mask one, mask two, reflecting you
Love bombing, clinging like *crazy* glue

When they don't approach, neither should you
Let them stare, their intentions aren't true

No, they're not just "nervous" or "shy"
Leave that for children, not an adult guy

Outwardly friendly, their world within chaotic
A mind diabolical, faking sympathetic

It's all spiritual, their acts aren't new
Look to the past, millennia in review

From the very, many, ancient days of old
Learned all that glitters sure ain't gold

With the Words of Life, discernment unparalleled
Falsehood thrown down, the Truth upheld

The eyesight of an eagle, and a falcon in flight
Their mask dispelled by the glory of Yah's Light

When you've figured them out, then they scatter
Nowhere to be found, no longer a matter

THE MIND OF FOLLY

Many minds remain unkind,
But Folly finds the foolish mind

Folly walks with foolishness,
Rejecting Light, fools choose darkness

They love ignorance and the wayward way,
Hating Truth and preferring to stay

In the mix of politricks, fictitious news and false reviews,
The cycle of drama and negativity choose

That's how they like it, it's how they exist
Their fuel for life, an impulsive tryst

A rendezvous with the death of the soul
Unknowing but knowing, darkness their goal

Wisdom beckons from city's high knoll
Calling to them as discordant bells toll

"To the Folly found and the folly bound,
To free you from foolishness why I came down,

To give you knowledge and a fighting chance
A higher Way, a soul-full dance

New life to revive, new gifts ensure
A hope for the present, abundance restore

Would you know Truth, do you desire Light?"
Wisdom inquired, waiting day and night

But those bells never stopped their clamoring,
The folly bound with clappers a-hammering

A continual utterance, wanting nothing to do with Her,
Preferring Madness and Folly remain their master

Let them alone, hope in time they'll learn
When that will be, only Yah can discern

LIFTED THE VEIL

Walking in ignorance, having no knowledge
Eyes blind, on a tight rope over Babel-ing bridge

Generational curses, bloodline polluted
Formed by witchcraft, by rebellion recruited

Couldn't get ahead, chaos their master
Year after year, one loss after another

A choice made to get to the root,
The source of misfortune bearing fruit

Mind was a hold of foul spirits and caged, unclean bird
But faith came by hearing, life quickened by the Word

The Truth washed and cleansed the fettered soul
Whom the enemy robbed, whose abundance he stole

Living in obedience, night and day
No longer a vagabond, no desire to stray

When the veil lifted,
The night by the Light sifted,

All kinds of creatures were found free
Caught by Truth, ending their liberty

Gargoyles and locusts, swarms in number
By the Word arrested, parted asunder

A discordant lot they were, set on destruction
Of the one alive, while dying in dysfunction

He sent them to the abyss by His command
The whole lot howling, while being disband

No other like Yahuah, His Word or His Spirit,
Oh, what deliverance, what undeserved merit!

All esteem to the One Who lifted the veil,
Who saved the soul, Whose Truth prevailed!

KEYS

Initiated under shackles of destruction,
under lying lips and systemic corruption,

and a psychosis of the heart, mind and soul.
You were asleep with eyes open when given goals.

Believing them to be your own,
you strove. Dedication was shown

for a determined destination, a place where
once found, a part of the mirage became clear.

But by some strange amnesia to what was obvious,
your mind reeled at the dubious, becoming delirious

as it recalibrated to save you from pain and anguish.
Truth entered, but you chose delusion and a wish

to remain in the lie. Deceiving yourself about the choice,
you danced a tango with death, ignoring Truth's Voice

and call for deliverance. The Keys to the Door
leading out of the maze were believed to be lore

as the heavens within awaited your desperate plea
to flee from falsehood (the iron bars that be

the thought strongholds of the mind). Truth flows
above the cyclical sea, calling still, while lies billow

from vortices below. "You simple one," Wisdom cries out,
"How long will you love simplicity?" Her shout

is heard by a few who awaken from self-deception
and come to know the Word of Truth. Their reception

of His Keys to the kingdom allow them unlimited access
to transcendence, to peace, to the Higher Mind, and a rest

from their wayward thoughts and fears. Then, upon entering
within, they are welcomed and enveloped in love everlasting

AUTHENTICITY

Hey, are you living true?
Tell me, please. Who are you?

Do you even really know?
Satisfied you seem with the whole show

Remember, you weren't always like this
As an unfettered child, imagination was bliss

With the time and storms of this existence
The real you struggled to hold up resistance

To the false, empty show they put on,
Forcing it, pretending to be strong

Appearing "weak," to them a detriment
Grin and bear it while allowing mistreatment

Covert relationships, expert showmanship
The bells and whistles of a lethal trip

Into the night, the growing darkness inside
The Truth you stifled, the real you hide

Dysfunction multiplied, falsehood galore
Pain and suffering, an increasing store

Unprecedented anxiety, calamity of the mind
The Words of Light entered, the darkness to bind

A stable mind on Truth founded
The only way to be grounded

This world will never agree
But within yourself content be

Most don't even really love themself
No longer be pressured into changing yourself

In the end, they'll all realize
This world and its trappings were never the prize

REFLECTIONS

With higher frequencies come new vision,
an elevated mental plane after your decision

to leave what wasn't serving Life behind.
Deceptive desires, part of the old mind,

were the body of death you parted with.
This accompanied by fictitious myths

of a world that intentionally had been
tampered with — all the lies they spin

concerning reality and how things came to be.
With the mind of Truth you're able to see

the many delusions created about existence.
They present a fiction and place for pretense

a fantasy while calling it science,
their many falsehoods, having no conscience.

Saying, "As above, so below,"
but as within, without they show

it cannot be the expectation that vapid shells
would produce Truth-Light from empty wells.

Neither would arid deserts have reliability
to produce waters for the weak and the thirsty.

Beings are reflections of what they carry within.
You cannot expect living Words from a rusty tin.

If only that tin has been tempered,
making it stronger, with usefulness rendered,

then you can have faith, the substance of hope—
no more in darkness ever to grope—

of a journey in a new world, one without end,
in which joy, peace, love and Light extends

PARAMOUNT PERCEPTIONS

What you perceive is what you'll receive,
Playing a key role in how you achieve

Perception skewed is the source of suffering
Misalignment, ill-content, the mind wandering

To and fro in constant motion
Life in this realm like waves of the ocean

The highest of crests and the lowest of troughs
Mind, will and emotions—steady then off

If you desire to rise, to remain above it all,
Seek Oneness in Truth, eternal peace to install

Learning life's lessons, some harder than others
In the midst of the storms, remaining unbothered

Making sense of your world with none other beside
Truth as your beacon, the gate narrow not wide

Understanding that people come and go,
So never an attachment to the fleeting grow

Perception renewed, source of life eternal
New mind, new world, new city internal

Set on a high hill that can never be hid,
Light shining bright over their dark grid

A crown and a scepter, bestowed authority
To guard Yah's Way found trustworthy

The mind of Ha'Mashiach, one of humility
Reverence, duty and service, true liberty

As a man thinks in his heart, so is he
Of this Truth, more certain one can't be

Your perception is paramount, this know for sure
The mind in you is the world you'll explore

UNTIL FULL DELIVERANCE

Cycles of dysfunction following generations
Increased self-awareness to bring true revelations

Self-defeating actions carrying to what end?
No benefit in sight, no reason to them defend

Why do you do it? You ask yourself repeatedly
What thoughts discordant, questioning belatedly

Moments in the midst, knowing you're in the wrong
And watching as if from outside as you go on

When the deed is done and you've fulfilled lust
You cower in shame, not even your own self to trust

Beating your chest, while asking Yah's forgiveness
To deliver you from the bondage, your self-imposed mess

Acknowledging you need help is the first step,
The higher mind fighting against dysfunction's depth

Wrestling against principalities and powers of the air,
The rulers of the darkness who won't your soul spare

Their desire is to have you, so master your flesh,
Pray for deliverance; you'll receive it at Yah's behest

Getting to the root of your cyclical deeds
Are they from you or from ancestral bloodlines received?

Any questions you have, ask the Spirit of Truth sincerely
And with focus and intention responses will come gradually

In the meantime, forgive yourself, moving on from sin's stain
This is the way of the righteous, in the pit do not remain

The renewal of your mind is a process as Light flows in
The past version of you dying, showing itself a rebellious twin

But Truth-Light is victorious no matter what it seems
Hold fast what you have, for as the chosen you're redeemed

THE SEASONS WITHIN

The ***fall*** is a descent into ego;
the pride of it all a vain show

It's where the physical and the visible
are what your mind deems credible

You are ruled by your emotions
and swayed by the many persuasions

of the five senses within your reality
In ***winter***, the finite tamps down on eternity

With this loss of true consciousness,
darkness and death come to harness

the life of the one walking in ignorance
It's a cold, calculated, trancelike dance

where transcendent love becomes the lake frozen
over, leaving life buried deep below the broken

depths within. You await the coming ***spring***
in which Truth-Light arrives, bringing

healing in His wings. The burgeoning heat
of the Words of Life ushers the soul's retreat

to come to an end. You are quickened,
made alive, as the flowers of your spirit are given

room to bloom and to grow. With ***summer***
fast approaching, the soul's glimmer

of hope crescendoes into full faith. The lake
frozen long ago is now a flowing stream. You take

many moments of silence, listening to the still,
small voice within. With this utterance of the will

of the Higher Mind into a new world guiding,
you are gifted transcendence and an eternal knowing

SUDDEN SHIFT

No one tells you, but it's true
Your life becomes what you value

Fixed attention on nothing besides
What's around turns to what's inside

It's otherworldly what you'll see
The way earth is meant to be

Co-creators with the Elohim of One
Who gave to us the Word, His Son

This new mind birthed from the Truth,
Which was hidden and kept from you

Blanketed by the darkness of falsehood
Your obedience to the Word the night withstood

That errant blindness is shattered now
As you remain loyal to your vow

To forever walk in the Word's Way
With no desire to ever stray

When suddenly, miracles arise
Your needs and wants materialize

As you abide in the Father's will,
And His Kingdom seek even still

Without words to describe what's happening
The Holy Spirit moving and providing

First a burst, and then some more
The heavenlies open as Yah restores

Everything the enemy had stolen
While you'd been lost, destitute and broken

Some seven, some ten, others a hundred-fold
To be returned, for the system can no longer withhold

NO OTHER VOICE

Eloquent speech fails to describe
the majesty of the One inside.

Neither lofty man, no matter how high,
could dare attempt to ever come nigh

the beauty, love and kindness of our King.
To Him a new song does our heart sing

in manifold witness of His Word, His character
and His mind. The eternal One, the Father,

to Whom comparable is no other, supplies all
and every need of those whom He calls

and chooses. In a depth of loving intimacy
are we with the Giver of true ascendancy

This love is not lip service, but intent, will,
and action; a love entered into that fills

the entire soul. The express manifestation
of which is shown forth as a demonstration

of resolute obedience to Him. An Emperor
of emperors, King of kings, Ruler of rulers,

Lord of lords is Yahuah El Shaddai,
the El Elyon of the heavens, earth, sea and sky

Never-ending worlds are His domain
His Light of Truth ever to remain,

flowing and extending in peace eon upon eon
He is seated on His throne, and knees we go on,

casting the crowns of our heads to the ground
His Voice resounds from the shamayim as the sound

of many waters. No other Voice as beautiful have we ever
 heard
Oh, Yahuah, by Your Presence are we forever reassured

THE MIND ANOINTED

Truth is the beacon of this mind, the Light
of the program within. Of renewed might

is this garden of the anointed. Faith arise!
Make the trees of this garden increasingly wise,

and humility, a paramount basis,
build up by their continual service

They join in an ode to the growth of brotherly love,
love for Abba and for the realms above

An obedience to the Word never behind,
while the knowledge of Most High does chaos bind

The Spirit of love, power
and a sound mind set to devour

the lack of understanding, followed
by transcendence through the Word hallowed

A countenance of contentedness
is coupled with unparalleled restfulness,

evidence of a peace that the outside will never understand
A patience and great grace one can only *inner*-stand

Kindness now means more than just a smile,
and gentleness more than the meek and mild

Self-control is another byproduct of the new programming,
the goodness from the higher planes no longer condemning,

but affording sharp discernment to the quickened soul;
and healing all waywardness, refining like purified gold

Forever placed in this mind's garden to tend and to keep it,
guarding the Word of Truth, a duty never to forfeit

The anointed mind is a world without end,
with Yah, the El of Peace, eternity to spend

THE JOURNEY WITHIN

The most important journey is the one within
The quest of a lifetime when awareness begins

To get there is a struggle, distractions abound,
Keeping you from yourself, their noise all around

Unlimited subscriptions, instant gratification,
"New" music and "entertainment," an entire fabrication

To take you from your own mind and into the world's,
The mind that never satisfies, emptiness unfurled

Finally, stopped to wonder, "Will it ever be enough?"
Why you're not happy, and still in *need* of more stuff

Being conscious of that much is a step toward the truth
Toward the core of everything, the very heart of you

The next step is simple, but may seem daunting
Especially if you find being in solitude haunting

Rising to the challenge as the quiet swells
Alone while you silence everything else

Go into the secret place as the Voice of Truth calls
The still, small Voice, not a shout nor a squall

Whispering words of life, a quickening essence
Reviving the soul, a reforming transcendence

A posture of reverence fostered as time goes by
Gratitude and humility, healing flowing as you cry

All the Words of Wisdom that Yahuah has said
Storing them up within the crown of your head

Not just your head but the heart of your mind,
The seat of your soul, throne of the Divine

No truer Word did one ever find
Darkness did it conquer, falsehood did it bind

THE EXTERNAL WAVE

Thrust, up, up, down, thrust, up, up, down,
A teaching, a learning, never left to drown

Under the high crests, lofty as they may be
My Father and I, Spirit of Truth leading me

In the midst of the lows, complete surrender
Never abandoned, guarded by my Defender

The Keeper of my mind, emotions, and will
Forever and ever abiding with me still

Simple yet beautiful is the eternal wave
Oneness with peace without end crave

A sweet melody and gentle lullaby
The thought of which makes me cry

A dream, a vision upon my bed
The healing stream to my soul is fed

A flow of tears and a soul deep sound
Emerging from within, companionship found

Oh, what delight this unfurled mystery!
Alone and separate will I never be

Soul's true Lover, in the center of my heart
From Whom I desire to never be apart

This world may find being in Peace boring
The One Whose Presence the mind finds calming

No physical thing could ever compare
To the One within Whom I hold dear

Of all that is in every realm of life, the Creator
My Beloved most kind, most beautiful, most pure

In this eternal wave of the highest frequency
Humble in radiance and sublime serenity

PEACE IN FLOW

"Ye, ye, ye, ye, ye, na-na-na-na"
I hear You, Abba

"Ye, ye, ye, ye, ye, na-na-na-na"
Enraptured in Yahuah

Peace is multiplied, a love so deep, so wide
Moments of silence within as waters slide

Deep calls unto deep, as the still voice seeps
Outward from Source, the One who my soul keeps

"Ye, ye, ye, ye, ye, na-na-na-na"
In love with my Abba

"Ye, ye, ye, ye, ye, na-na-na-na"
Oneness with Yahuah

In quietness and rest, He is my confidence,
Growing in strength as inside takes residence

A house set on a hill, a fortified city
Truth-Light masters darkness, taking no pity

"Ye, ye, ye, ye, ye, na-na-na-na"
I'm walking with Abba

"Ye, ye, ye, ye, ye, na-na-na-na"
Esteem to Yahuah

He caught the robbers of my soul, now stopped from doing so
Thieves found and time's up, oh, woe, woe, woe

Plunderer is plundered, the way it has to be
No greater salvation, but for them calamity

"Ye, ye, ye, ye, ye, na-na-na-na"
Grateful am I, Abba

"Ye, ye, ye, ye, ye, na-na-na-na"
No one like You, Yahuah

A THING CALLED "BEAUTY"

In the heavens, the realms above
Beauty is a product of Love

Beauty comes from Truth's inner glow
Not one part nor parcel is a vain show

In the world within, the purity of Beauty
Comes not from the outward looks' obscurity

It emanates from the heart of the soul
Righteous character the rule, the ultimate goal

Without depth of meaning and life's true purpose
Beauty becomes like a cyclical circus

Changing outer shells every few years
While the soul inside dies, overcome with fears

The being becomes a farce, a lightbulb without Light
A malfunctioning lamp, useless in the night

Because the focus wasn't the core
The soul writhes, withers, suffers sore

To the outside world of this plane below
Beauty defined by the flesh's vapid glow

Purpose exchanged for competition
Crabs in a bucket without true elevation

As their "status" increases so do their lies
And the inexorable emptiness they feel inside

They try to escape this through their parties,
Alcohol, drugs, and continual debaucheries

Hoping their rebellion will fill the void,
Knowing well that to death they're joined

"Party on," they cry out, killing Truth's Beauty,
And to their souls committing utter cruelty

LIKE SIFTED, SHIFTING SANDS

Like shifting sands through the glass of time
Many change at the drop of a dime

A dime a dozen is how they come and go,
Mostly fickle, their lives a staged show

A show for accolades, "bravo," "hooray"
Fearing dislike and from others dismay

Dismay for how they are inside
Diabolical mind, filled with self-centered pride

Pride at the ready to burst from its seams
With wicked winks and mischievous schemes

These schemes they naturally with thought invent
For the unassuming soul whose mind they rent

Rents they inflict, committing psychological violence
Hiding in plain sight, while avoiding recompense

But recompense comes on swift wings
Eternal justice from within the Truth rings

Ringing aloud and crying out in wrath against the insanity
Of the covert acts that destroy the harmony of humanity

Humanity in their everlasting home and abode of peace
That existed before the pompous ones' release

They released toxicity, into the environment leaking
Enticing others to act in the way of self-seeking

But self-seeking destroys the soul within, the pure, gifted essence

Throwing the soul and entire being out of balance

And if balance be no more, no longer can one explore
True beauty of all becomes an eyesore as the egoic mind fills
    the core

Many choose the egoic, forever in darkness to be
Like sifted sands beneath the cyclical sea

TO LOVE AN ENEMY I

"Love your enemies, and pray for those who
persecute you," said the Word. This you must do

"so that you may be the sons of your Father in heaven,"
forgiving your enemies seventy times seven.

I did not really understand what it meant
to love an enemy, but with Yah much time I spent

as the Holy Spirit guided me;
a revelation leading to true liberty.

For you to know how this truly goes
requires understanding of how love flows,

while living with a new and transformed mind.
At first uncomfortable, but in time you'll find

that loving an enemy naturally pours forth
from the inside of you. It won't be about their worth

as *you* see it, but about the Truth that they have
their being also in the Father. He created vessels of

honor and vessels of dishonor, and made
rain fall on the just and the unjust. Because you laid

up treasures in the heavens, you've received gifts
from the Word of Yah, chief among them a shift

in mentality. From the inside core, you can love,
much like the Father of Lights within and above.

This love transcends the carnal attitudes of offense,
and holds all in full view of Truth. Without pretense

or partiality, judging thoughts and intentions
of the heart, you perceive all spirits through actions,

words, and energy. From this vantage point
with the eyes of the Spirit of Truth, an heir joint

TO LOVE AN ENEMY II

We're joint with the Prince of Peace whose mind we
inherit when in Oneness with the Father. You see,

with time and through your healing,
love flows from you. It isn't simply a feeling

but a genuine care for fellow beings and the earth
herself. From the Word of Truth, this powerful rebirth

will engender a transformative perspective.
Your "enemy" becomes a lesson on how to live

with opposition, overcome trials and resist
temptation. You'll understand why toxic people exist.

The trials with these vessels represent a furnace
of cleansing. Through this refinement process

of interfacing with your "enemy," you learn forgiveness,
boundaries, and patience as Yah purges your soul's dross.

You're likened to clay in the Potter's hand for a reason.
The Father fashions you, knowing the appointed season

in which you'll show forth the praises and esteem of the One
Who brought you out of darkness into Light. His Son,

the Living Word, triumphs in Truth through you and
defeats all your "enemies," strengthening you to withstand

their attacks and remain L.O.V.E.[1] He doesn't allow

---

1. L.O.V.E. - Living in Oneness Vs. Ego

vitriol and hatred to change your purity and vow

to be obedient to His will and purpose for your life.
Through moments of heartache, disillusionment and strife,

you persist in love, hope and resilience. You do what's right
even when others may backbite, envy and slight.

This conclusion is the score: You love your
"enemy" by abiding in Oneness and Truth forevermore.

SOUNDNESS OF MIND

'Twas a world of ups and downs,
a cyclical sea of smiles and frowns

The unsteady nature of such darkness
left emotions an unpredictable mess

with no self-control and an inability to rise
above the foolishness. Thinking yourself wise

you continued on in madness and folly,
following delusion and pretending to be jolly

While your mind, in delirium, created a landscape
as a means of self-soothing, a way of escape

from the pains and anguish of reality. Truth
beckoned. The Word called you to the root,

to the core and Source of you, to the One Who
magnanimously heals, and Whose healing is true,

lasting forevermore. The Father abundantly pardons
once your heart is no longer hardened,

but open to His Way of Oneness and righteousness
In this life-giving relationship, lovingkindness

is imparted through the Holy Spirit with power,
and with many other gifts are you showered

Soundness of mind is an essential one you're promised
the moment your egoistical mind you relinquish,

never to look back. Rose-tinted glasses
are gone as sobriety of spirit greatly surpasses

the lack of power and understanding from before
Your affection set on the world within, a restored

position in the heavenlies, of which you glean
peace. No other mind possesses a life so serene

LOVERS IN LIGHT

The ones who love tell the truth
They would never deceive you

Yes, at times, they may seem blunt
In keeping you from evil's hunt

Don't hate the ones who are like me
We know no other Way to be

Than to live in honesty
In this world's cyclical sea

Where all falsehoods come and go,
A short-lived lie, a vapid show

We desire you to remain
Your conscience clear, without a stain

To be among the meek
Who the new earth seek

A higher life, a better Way
Never in darkness ever to stay

Therefore, the Truth we venerate
To heal the mind, to elevate

Transcending webs of thought
That together bring to naught

Words of Life are the Key
Open door to victory

A higher mind, a brighter Day
No more lies to hold sway

Over the final destiny
Of whom the ones in Truth see

Trimming the lamp, fighting the fight
Nothing as true as the lovers in Light

GUARD YOURSELF

Guard your heart with every diligence,
for from it flows life's existence

The choices you make are of the utmost importance,
and the company you keep vital to the balance

of your soul's inner core, the Spirit of life within
Vanity and falsehood with a cart rope is drawn sin,

a dysfunctional way of life leading to emptiness,
a sense of loss, and feeling meaningless

Guard yourself, many aren't loyal
Guard yourself, or they could become lethal

"Misery loves company" is not a cliche
Draw hard boundaries if you desire not to stray

into the den of wolves feening for your life's blood
Seeing the light in you, they come in like a flood;

a whirlwind of darkness cut off from the Father,
the only Source of abiding life. They gather

around you to siphon your spirit-energy, but don't
let them! A parasitic nature is their core, so they won't

be able to reciprocate anything you give
They are takers, knowing only to receive

If they give, it's only for self-seeking ends
Watch their energy and spend

time observing how you feel with them. If left in confusion,

questioning reality, leave their folly and self-inflicted
    delusion

Fix your mind on the Most High for just and true is His Way
Guard yourself in reverence and to Him forever say,

"Abba, in all existence, only You are holy"
Truly, of all your love and reverence only Yah is worthy

LOVE LETTER TO THE TRUTH

They say You hurt, but to me that pain is good
I'd rather live in You than die under falsehood

You came to me as a gentle, still, small Voice,
Instructing in the Way and allowing me free choice

Your high frequency of Light saved me from being perpetual prey
From parasites, vampires, from dysfunction and soul's dismay

When I made the decision to come into full alignment,
Walking in True reality, with Wisdom was no more estrangement

The electromagnet within turned, attuned to Your Kingdom
Stopped seeking what didn't satisfy as I was joined to True freedom

Oh, what deliverance! What loving, peace, and humbling service,
Living in Truth and in the earth working righteousness

The darkness that had a foothold, relinquished all in defeat
No soul's energy to harness, no more life-force to eat

Oh, Truth, You are most beautiful, as are Your next of kin
Wisdom, Love, Justice, Knowledge and Understanding

I used to envy the birds, the cattle and the horses
How simply they lived without lies and artifices

'Twas not until Truth beckoned within the core of my own spirit
Said I too once lived carefree with eternal joy and intrinsic merit

I was called to return to the True Lover of my soul
The Everlasting Oneness Who encompasses and fills all

The Way, the Truth, the Life was the One I thirsted for,
Searching with all my heart in a stillness like never before

The Most High, in those moments, drew ever nearer still
    to me
Truth, You were poured forth, bringing me up from the
    cyclical sea

When my eye became single, Your pristine House within my
    stay,
I made a vow to forever guard myself, that is Truth, come
    what may

At Oneness in Truth without end forevermore.

> "But when He comes, the Ruah [Spirit] of Truth, He shall guide you into all the truth."
>   John 16:13a

> "And you shall know the truth, and the truth shall make you free."
>   John 8:32

EVENING

In the dead of night
When many stars give their light
The fallen do fight

MORNING

At the break of day
No place found for them to stay
Abysmal dismay

CHAOS

Confusion's the test
Inconsistency its nest
Never finding rest

PEACE

An eternal flow
No longer tossed to and fro
To be still and know

NIGHT.

Darkness ... deceiver
Higher Mind is still Ruler
I Am its Keeper

DAY

Called the Word of Truth
In Oneness and justice rule
None compare to You!

DARKNESS

Delusions and lies
Rejected Truth, blinded eyes
Remaining unwise

LIGHT

When Truth has entered
Soul once caged, now a free bird
All falsehood interred

PRIDE

Ego on the rise
Inflated pride in disguise
In this the soul dies

PURPOSE

An eternal life
Neither pompousness nor strife
Oneness fully rife

HELL

In the grip of fear
'Tis when ignorance is near
A void called despair

HEAVEN

In love, perfected
Eternal peace, transcended
The mind, enlightened

WITHOUT

Seeking with the eyes
That which never satisfies
As "lack" underlies

WITHIN

Oneness is the rest
Kingdom of heaven access
Abundance mindset

ILLUSION

Birth is the en-trance
Into 3D's bad romance
Starts the ego's dance

REALITY

Delusions deny
Truth lives and the ego dies
As Light fills the eye

DOWN

**Magnetic forces
Dark duress pulls and pushes
Blind consciousnesses**

UP

Drawn to Yah Most High
They chose the Light not the lie
Told ego, "Bye-bye"

FALSEHOOD

Egocentric mind
Many fantasies fools find
Made folly their grind

TRUTH

The mind authentic
Chose no delusion, nor tricked
Escaped the gimmick

DESTRUCTION

Chaos, their order
The vessels of dishonor
That is their nature

CREATION

The order of One
Vessels of honor, Light's Son
Victory they've won

AUTUMN'S WINTER

Autumn leaves turn brown
The dead and dying fall down
Winter's found, no crown

SPRING'S SUMMER

Spring flowers appear
When newness of life draws near
Summer's triumph cheer

BELOW.

In the pit they've dug
Instability, cruel drug
Wild locusts, their bug

ABOVE

Life everlasting
A stable mind is their spring
Let the praises ring!

WASTE PLACE

A bottomless hole
Where souls' energy they stole
None offered console

FRUITFUL FIELD

Realm with much in store
Abundance forevermore
As the minds explore

DESERT

**Detected devils
Come to waste souls by evils
Malignant perils**

LIVING SPRING

The waters of Life
Flow forth to save souls from strife
Emergent Truth-Light

ONENESS

"It is done!" Lies fled
All enemies put to bed
Nothing left unsaid

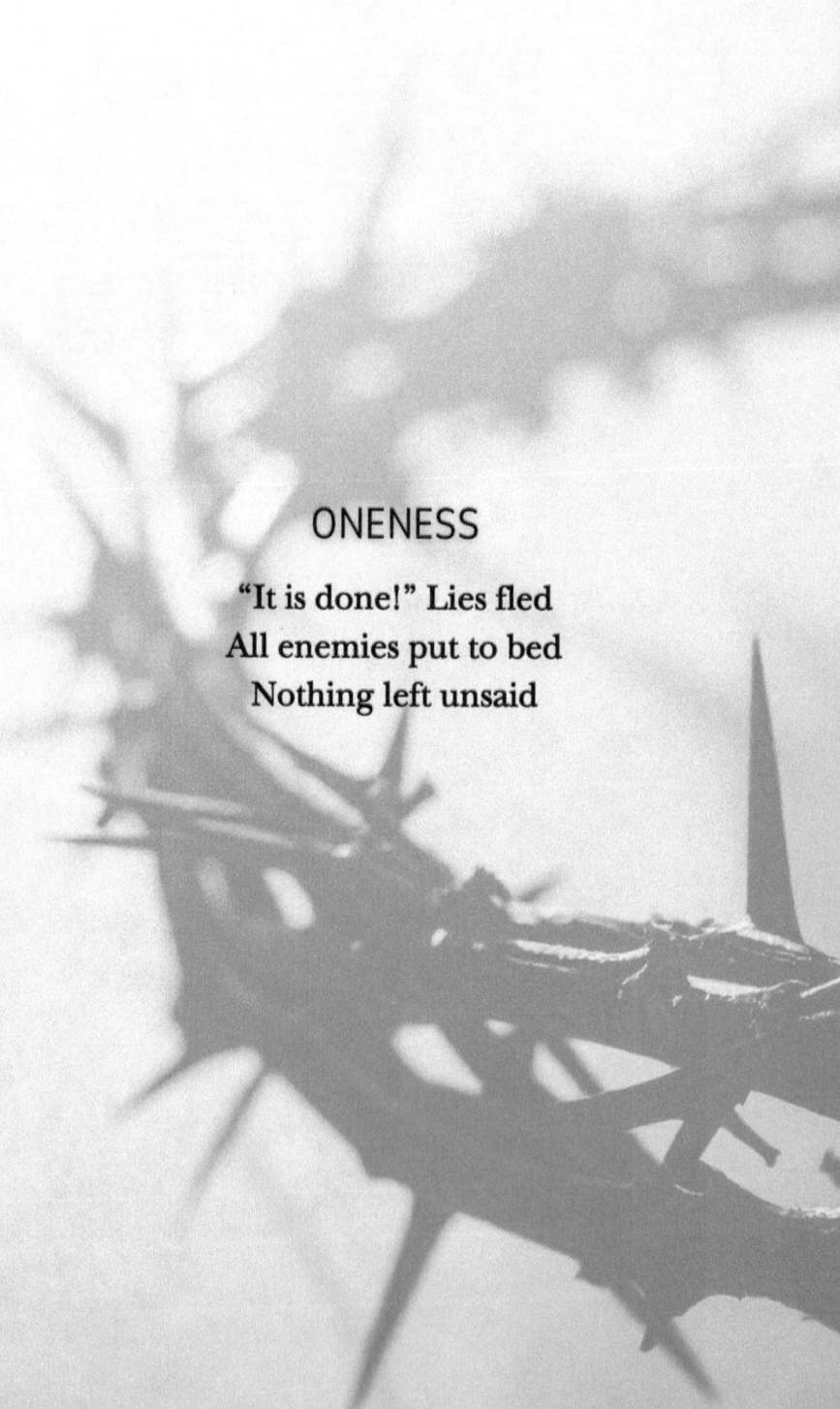

ONENESS

"It is done!" Lies fled
All enemies put to bed
Nothing left unsaid

UPROOTING
UNCONSCIOUSNESS

UPROOTING

Once blind, lost in the dark abyss
Awake, yea, arise, oh sleeper
A wish to be taken deeper
Enlightened, falsehood found amiss

A QUICKENING

Rebirth in the dearth of the earth
Parched place of dry ground needs water
Flows at the will of its caller
Now a Truth mindset makes alert

POMPOUS FUTILITY

Though try and try and try they might
There is no one like the Most High
In all earth, the sea and the sky
Fools never *ever* reach His height

LET THEM ALONE

The fool says, "There's no Elohim"
Realm of words, one of energy
From which they glean life's synergy
Yet, die they from sheer pride-esteem

KEY CALLED HUMILITY

Humble yourself in His presence
Venerate the Truth-Light Healer
of your soul. Maker and Keeper,
Him, in humility, reverence.

DESOLATE HOUSES

    The spirit of man has a house
    If left unguarded, thieves enter
    Lower entities, no order
    They steal light; emptiness aroused

THOSE OF THE VOID

    They rejected the Truth, Light's Son
    Hate whom they can't manipulate
    And then try to triangulate
    They are the enemies of One

NO CONTROL

A sailing ship with no captain
Is the one without self-control
Subconscious subverted, new role
Sunken place in which they remain

SHARK-INFESTED WATERS

While down in the cyclical sea
Duality of black and white,
Many making the soul contrite
You and I, within let's journey

PRACTICING LAWLESSNESS

    The way you live is how you'll end
    Dedicated to dysfunction
    With no other soul compulsion
    Cycles of eternity spend

DYSFUNCTION AND DELIRIUM

Making up their rules as they go
Defying Truth, against the right
Deep love and oneness out of sight
Aloud they cry, "On with the show"

SCRIPTED LIFE

On autopilot life may seem
Running on a program within
Subconscious choices they siphon
Eyes open, but feels like a dream

SOUL FRUITS

    Gleaning from the Holy Spirit
    From within, healed soul's true function
    What's right, what's good, set in motion
    Eternal flow's fruitful merit

THE WAY OF PRIDE

There's no such thing as their own way
But folly, darkness and the void,
While making themself sin's android
And changing to Night what was Day

ANDROIDS OF CHAOS

Do you know from where chaos stems?
Frequency low, no self-control
Darkness stepped into its new role
As lower minds sing its anthem

WISDOM'S DAUGHTERS

Minds guarded from falsehood and lies
Enlightened by Truth, their Keeper
And while loyal to no other
The wickednesses they despise

ENTRAPMENT

Of this we are not ignorant —
The ego and its devices
From which all the artifices
Have origin and entrenchment

LIGHT ESTEEMED!

"Taste! See that the Adon is good."
Oh, I have tasted and have seen
None like Yahuah Elohim!
I cut off folly and falsehood

MIND, WILL, EMOTIONS

What's the soul of humanity?
It originates in Spirit
Giving the mind all its merit,
Emotions, will and clarity

SPIRIT OF TRUTH

An intelligent Energy
Transcending, teaching, uplifting
A peaceful flow everlasting
Encompassing eternity

TRUST

Hand held by the Eternal One
As we learn from the Higher Mind
Continual growth and Truth find
His Spirit never abandons

SUBCONSCIOUS JOURNEY

    Awareness tends to come slowly
    This-and-that triggers. Who triggers?
    Pain as a new question lingers
    Soon, understanding dawns gently

TREE OF LIFE

    Truth, eternal Word, life-giving
    Enlightening the spirit man
    Beckoning entire lifespans
    The unseen and true El within

TREE OF GOOD AND EVIL

    Made unto corruptible flesh
    "I (eye) see men like trees walking"
    Ego mind of the 3D ring
    Pulls at the soul to him enmesh

DEEP WAVES

In the stillness, His Voice is heard
A peaceful Sound, One to hallow
No other to laud nor follow
There is only the Good Shepherd

RADICAL ACCEPTANCE

Sometimes confused with giving up
It's the acknowledgement of Truth
Even when it doesn't suit you
A growth in consciousness once stuck

DRACONIAN CRONIES

They are blind leaders of the blind
Working to create craftiness
Siding with evil they love best
Their final prize — unstable mind

DEFEATED IN DISCOVERY

    Does another *son* bite the dust?
    It will not happen on My watch
    Soul's foe, that draconian wretch
    Is whom they'll never again trust

SUBCONSCIOUS HEALED

Gone are the wounds, bruises and sores
The past had complete burial
At Oneness in Truth eternal
Spirit man keeping no more score

TOTAL RENEWAL

Forgave, having been forgiven
L.O.V.E.[1] for His Word gave me power
In the *now*, I'm set forever
Free from the cyclical prison

---

1. L.O.V.E. - Living in Oneness Vs. Ego

THE WORD

OF LIFE

KADOSH NAME

The Word
New beginning
Quickening, life-giving
Breath of the Almighty spoken
I Am

STILL, SMALL VOICE

"Be still."
Whisper within
Prompting, "This is the Way
Walk therein and you'll find pasture"
I do

HIGHEST FREQUENCY

Of Light
Mind vibration
Purity, peace and life
What's right and good; Holy Spirit
Of Truth

ANOTHER WORLD

    Higher
    A world within
    Realm of pure Light and Truth
    No night there, only day, having
    No end

MIND WITHIN

    Of Christ
    Fully awake
    Risen high above all
    Principalities and powers
    Kept crown

WELL-LIT LAMP

    Knowing
    Truth multiplied
    Intense beacon of Light
    Filled with the ever-present El
    Shaddai

TRUTH IS LIGHT

The Way
Darkness scatters
Overruled by what's right
Falsehood cast into the abyss
For Good

PERSONHOOD

    Light Is
    A Being with
    His own High Form in realms
    Invisible to the fleshly
    Mind's eye

TRUTH-LIGHT TO VISIBLE LIGHT

Came down
Word was made flesh
Showed the Way for His own
Gained the victory over sin
Went up

WORD OF ELOHIM

Yah's Voice
In the heavens
Riding on cherubim,
On the wings of the wind, His Word
Thunders

EXPOSED DARKNESS

Falsehood
Revealed by Truth
Made aware of trauma
Pride and ego now naked, bare
Destroyed

SOVEREIGN'S CONTROL

    Most High
    El Elyon
    In ultimate control
    Exalted above all the earth
    Abba

CONQUERED FEAR

Fear was
A weapon formed
But it did not prosper
'Twas used to exert force, control
Cast out!

OCCUPIES THE ALTAR

    Enthroned
    Voice from within
    Flowing, emanating
    Exalted in the spirit man
    Pure Word

INDWELLING

Spirit
Holy union
Made alive, undefiled
Spirit man's house clean and varnished
Risen

ABOVE THE GRID

    Held high
    Above the fray
    In the eternal now
    Truth brings vision and clarity
    Timeless

IN THE HEAVENLIES

Drawn up
Into the Light
A kingly crown above
Humble adherence to Yah's Word
The Key

SHIFTED THE PARADIGM

Struggle
A wrestling
To break free from ego—
The lower mind that held sway. *Now*,
We're free

TRUE INTIMACY

Oneness
Eternal flow
A teaching, a learning
Some lessons are easy, some hard
Training

TRANSCENDENCE

Vision,
Wisdom, foresight—
Gifts from the Word of Truth
Seeing into the unseen realms
Unmatched

ETERNALLY GUIDED

The Way
Of growth and healing
In alignment with Yah
Word of Light, Truth everlasting
Spoken

KADOSH COUNCIL

Throne room
"Whom do I send?"
Here am I, Adonai,
Living for the Vision within
Oneness

VISION

> Insight
> Presence rising
> Into the realms above
> Making the unseen visible
> Attuned

PURPOSEFUL PARTNERS

Allies
Forged in purpose
On earth as in heaven
Not our will but the Most High's done
In Truth

NO LOOKING BACK

    Onward
    To Mount Zion
    Lift up your face. Greet her
    Healing flows as she receives her
    Children

METAMORPHOSIS

    Enter
    Solitude, rest
    Cocooned in earth body
    Fleshly mind crucified. New mind
    In Christ

ONWARD, UPWARD

    Marching
    Eyes to the prize
    Holding fast to their crown
    Forward ever, backwards never
    The Way

DNA INSCRIBED

The Word
Eternal Truth
Written with Yah's finger
Now inscribed in our inward parts
Our Guide

SCROLL

    Loosened
    Unfurled within
    Revealing life's journey
    Thoughts, words, actions—every moment
    Judgement

BOOK OF LIFE

Chosen,
They spoke His Word
Purity their power,
Living on in Truth eternal
Enthroned

WORLD WITHOUT END

    Most High
    Priority
    Eon upon eon
    Their dwelling in Truth, in Oneness,
    In Rest

PIERCING THROUGH

THE VEIL

WHAT DO YOU SEEK?

In the search you may find
It's not about chasing what is without
It's about becoming who you truly are
Which in essence is pure love
All that you seek after, all that you need
Is already within you

WHAT YOU SEEK, SEEKS YOU

Looking for acceptance
Accept your own being
Looking for love
You already are
Looking for home
Go within

WHO ARE YOU?

In pondering this
You may respond with
Your familial connection
Your occupation
Your current relationship status
Are those indeed who you are?

YOU ARE WHO YOU ARE

    Here is the simple
    Yet true response
    You are here
    You are *now*
    You are ...
    You

WHO SEES YOU?

Hold the mirror up to yourself
Whom do you see?
Your neighbor?
A brother?
Or a friend, perhaps?
Tell me whom you see

YOU SEE YOU

    Multifaceted layers of humanity
    In many around you
    You see parts of yourself
    Oftentimes, mirrored back
    You see you in them
    It's true

WHO KNOWS YOU?

To be known
Or to know yourself
Which is the more important
Of the two?
Does anything truly matter
If *you* don't know you?

REMEMBER WHO YOU ARE

Time spent alone
In silence, and focused on the *now*
Remaining in Presence
The unknown will come
Falsehood will be dissolved by Truth
And you will know as you are known

WHERE ARE YOU?

Are you there?
Are you here?
The unmanifested
Manifested as separate hosts in the physical
Yet at Oneness, present everywhere
Filling and encompassing all

YOU ARE NOW?

What is *now*?
It is Presence
Energy in flow
A journey from and
To destinations unknown
Yet known

WHERE DO YOU COME FROM?

Fashioned in the womb
You entered the 3D
A long journey, yet a short one
From realm to realm
Formed there
"Physical" here

FROM THE REALMS UNSEEN

    Like roots which grow downward into earth
    So is your origin in the realm unseen
    You manifest in the physical like a tree planted,
    Whether by the rivers of the waters of life
    Or by a parched place,
    This is only known by the health of your fruit

WHY ARE YOU HERE?

You know
Don't doubt it
You were made to forget
When you entered the cyclical sea
Your purpose is found in alignment with Light
Seek Truth, because it's dark out there in the abyss

MEANING, PURPOSE

    Once aligned with Truth-Light
    A beacon of knowing enters
    A rebirth, a growth in spirit, quickening the soul
    Suddenly, understanding dawns
    Meaning springs forth
    Catapulting you into purpose

WHAT IS MEANING?

    Meaning is transcendence in L.O.V.E.[1]
    The essence of life
    Recognizing that every form has its intrinsic value
    And is part of the whole
    In realms seen and unseen
    Meaning is living out the pure essence of Oneness in Truth

---

1. L.O.V.E. - Living in Oneness Vs. Ego

WHAT IS PURPOSE?

Purpose is derived from meaning
It is an understanding of service
From one form to another
Flowing, realm to realm
Serving all, in all, for the greater Good
Purpose is characteristic of Truth-Light

WHERE ARE YOU GOING?

What is a "destination,"
And why is it considered such?
Who said once you've reach it
You've arrived at the end of the road,
At fulfillment?
What is "fulfillment?"

POSITIONING

Space, "time," location, realm
Reaching higher planes of awareness
Truth-Light consciousness
Approaching, knowing
"Fulfillment" is positioning,
Closer intimacy in Oneness with Truth and Life

WHAT DO YOU HEAR?

Are you able to discern the Voice
Within the cacophony all around?
Mixtures of frequencies
Attempt to distinguish themselves
Yet remain illusions of a single sound,
You listen, but none stands out

FREQUENCY OF SOUND, OF LIGHT

The frequency of *now* is only discernible
When you are still,
Causing ricocheting to cease
When there are no more echoes, no more refractions
The ubiquitous, unperturbed and unending,
Still, small Voice within is heard, is witnessed

WHAT IS IGNORANCE?

A lack of awareness
Creating blindness, weakness
A certain gullibility
A state of being easily manipulated
And a tending towards folly
Meeting of the mind with falsehood, chaos

BLINDNESS

    Darkness
    Enveloped in the cyclical abyss
    Where lack of learning, lack of growth
    Causes you to remain in the ignorance
    Of infancy indefinitely, though the body ages
    The mind is made a mental prison of delusion

WHAT IS DEATH?

Extremely low consciousness
A journey towards annihilation
Of the higher Self, of the Spirit, of the soul
Approximating the most low
The eye at the bottom
Of the pit

EXTREMELY LOW CONSCIOUSNESS

Frequencies nearing flatline
Cyclical existence — pride to shame, shame to pride
The depths of suffering, of anguish
Where chaos is order, force
Perpetual night, falsehood
In the trenches, midnight zone

WHAT IS LIFE?

Full Presence, Truth
Highest frequencies, meaning, purpose
Reciprocal existence — symbiosis
Abundance, joy, peace, eternal day
Power, transcendent love
Drawn to the highest heavens, realms above the seas

SPIRIT OF TRUTH

    Light frequency, entering,
    Piercing through the darkness,
    Tearing the veil, revealing
    Mysteries within the pure, repentant heart
    Truth casts out fear, perfecting the soul
    In transcendence, in L.O.V.E.[1]

---

1. L.O.V.E. - Living in Oneness Vs. Ego

WHAT IS FEAR?

Founded in ignorance, in falsehood
A delusion of the egocentric mind
Conceiving a nonexistent reality
It is formed by forces of the remnants of pride and folly
A product of rejected Truth, a spiritual death causing
A decent in consciousness, an energetic collapse

EGOCENTRIC MIND

A delusional and self-absorbed mindset
Fear-based, caused by a refusal to accept and honor Truth
This mind degrades the very principles that support life
It tends towards death — initially of spirit-energy
Before culminating in the soul's dysfunction and ruin
Eventually, the "physical" expires without hope

WHAT IS FREEDOM?

    Authenticity
    Daring to show up as *truth*
    In a world desiring you to be anything but
    Healing — choosing yourself, L.O.V.E.ing[1] yourself
    The eternal and Most High within
    Guarding Yah's Word of Truth in rest

---

1. L.O.V.E. - Living in Oneness Vs. Ego

TRUTH AND LIGHT

    Vital, intelligent, purest and highest energy
    Without beginning, having no end
    Reciprocal above, its opposition cyclical below
    Teaching and learning
    Forming and creating
    Eternal oneness, power

ENDED

THE STRIFE

RIDDANCE TO WELCOME

As ego dies, fades away, Life grows into the *true* Way.

A VOICE IN THIS PLACE

In a world pulling you into anything but, show up as Light.

PEACE

Internal, eternal flow from realms above, within.

ABSENCE, PRESENCE

Absent from the cyclical show; *now* present within, above.

CREATE MORE THAN CONSUME

Free from the world of too much consuming; fully crossed over to creating.

SUSTENANCE

Our food is to guard and to do righteousness and Truth.

TRUE REALITY

Truth embraced from the reign within gives insight, foresight and discernment.

ONE WITH TRUTH

When the Bright, Morning Star has dawned in your heart, you've been resurrected.

ACCORD

Atoned, attuned, aligned in You.

SELF-MASTERY

Branches well-pruned with a perpetual hedge of protection,
we eternally tend the fire on our altar.

AUTHENTIC AUTHORITY

Transcendent love, complete dedication, unwavering respect, honor and blessing to the Most High Yah above and over all things.

FULFILLMENT

Far above the waves, to a depth reached within, a great calm past defining resounds in Yah.

ALLEGIANCE

Unchangeable loyalty comes with deep awareness, a higher mind and intimacy with the Spirit of Truth.

ESTABLISHED

A knowing within that all things arrive in their appointed season

CONFIDENCE

Continual growth in spirit *is* the "laying up of treasures in heaven" of which *none* can bereave you.

A HIGHER PLANE

Another mind-world in which the principles of Truth, wisdom, righteousness, and peace reign eternally

MIND-WORLDS

Frequencies of perception, increasing as you journey deeper within

EYES

Perceptions of reality beyond that of the "physical," cyclical sea of the 3D

FOUR FACES

Perceptions and powers coupled with the wisdom to discern which best fits the occasion

EAGLE

Domain: heavens—higher realms; Powers: sight and flight

ADAM

Domain: earths—multiple realms; Powers: word and dominion

LION

Domain: beasts—authoritative realms; Powers: might and leadership

CHERUB

Domain: underworlds—service-oriented realms; Powers: brute force and sacrifice

WINGS

Transport and protection

RIGHT HAND

Power and authority

FEET

Position and jurisdiction

"OH, WHEEL"

A structure housing a spirit, moving only in accordance with the intent and will of that spirit

FIRMAMENT

A structure containing coded portals — keys are needed for specific spirits to pass through.

SERVICE

Purpose

REALM-TO-REALM

Appearing "here" and "there" without the limitations of "space" or "time"

FROM ABOVE

Life and Power in Truth and Oneness

OPPRESSORS

WEEP AND WAIL

GNASHING OF TEETH

Truth can be painful as the fantasy fades
The lacking in heart its realities evade,
Preferring to live in diabolical delusion,
While the resilient in heart accept Truth's revelation

Those eschewing wisdom, compassion and kindness
Remain in the dust of low consciousness,
Choosing to hide behind the opaque veil
Truth's many oppressors, they weep and wail

A CHOSEN DEATH

    Weeping and wailing and gnashing of teeth,
    They glare and scowl then cower in defeat
    It seems what they expected was to reign, but why?
    Who would allow their renewed rebellion on high?

    "Bow the knee," the judgment and off to the abyss below
    'Twas their choice and no others' — going with the most low
    What's crazy is if given another chance to repent
    They'd walk the same path, upholding evil's tent

CYCLICAL SEA

Doing the same things again and again
No learning never, in eternity to spend
Around and around is the cyclical show
On the merry-go-round, circuit of the most low

Reeling and wandering through the blackness of night
Chained in the darkness with each other to fight
No Light there, only death in store
No more Life, nothing new to explore

DARK ALIGNMENT

Siding with wickedness then sent to the abyss
No mistaking it, their ego found nothing amiss
They chose darkness, and it filled their soul's core
Light was rejected and desired no more

Yah Most High had placed eternity in their heart
A decision of positioning for the soul's will from the start
To either dwell on high or sink into the most low
Their alignment deciding which destiny was bestowed

CITY'S ENEMIES DEFEATED

They surrounded City, hoping to destroy her crown of glory
Dragon and his cronies, casting lies, fear and fury
But for her my Beloved upheld His Shield of protection
The Word of Truth, His standard against their corruption

Fully aligned through the Prince of Peace, Christ Yeshua
City's mighty citadel now under the shadow of Yahuah
The fire of His presence incinerated her foes
Angels herald to earth's inhabitants, "Woe! Woe! Woe!"

DECOYS OF THE NIGHT

The spectrum of flesh hiding ghouls inside
Their strange force and flame they couldn't hide
Vampiric, parasitic, contrary to Life
Chaos they loved and created strife

Appearing in the realm of day and night,
The decoys of darkness sought to steal and kill Light
Unsuccessful in achieving their devilish goal
The abyss they chose rose to consume their soul

ALIVE BUT DEAD

Watchers, oh watchers, listen you of the Day
Dawn has arisen but others went their own way
When asked repeatedly to rise or to die
Twisted faces in rebellion the following they did cry

"Watchers, oh watchers, hear us you of the Night
Your rewards we have chosen and made them our might"
They rejected Truth-Light to satisfy their own flesh
And in the world of darkness their minds they enmeshed

ILLUSIONS OF SEPARATION

Bedlam of darkness, spectrum of the most low
Where lies and self-centeredness is all they know
From one corner of the earth stretching to another
Signs n' symptoms of devils the whole world over

A hive mind, the lot of them, seeking only pleasures, superficial
Thinking they're unique, different, amazing and special
Are they, though? No, you just wait, watch and see
They all do the same thing in the dark, cyclical sea

VORTICES OF CHAOS

There they go, the diabolical deviants
Controlled souls in the flesh of "giants"
The "greats" of the world, entitled "men of renown"
Putting themselves on "thrones" without eternal crowns

What they meant for evil has been turned to good
Unintended teachers existing in every falsehood
Vortices of chaos with infinite vacuums within
Tormentors tormented by their own bodies of sin

THE TECHNOLOGY OF FLESH

Contrary to the Spirit of Truth
Its mechanisms meant to deceive you
The flesh, wired and contrived ego
System with low consciousness tangled

Fearful, vengeful, with jealousies filled
Strife, sedition, by darkness willed
The technology of flesh, a world of rebellion
The moon, its heart, blackened by delusion

BALANCING THE UP AND DOWN

Two worlds collide on the plane called earth
Realm within realms, births within birth
Some filled with Truth, others steeped in falsehood
The Light and the darkness on "solid" ground stood

A game board of sorts, the people its players
Above playing Go, beneath Chess, still others Checkers
The stage of Day and Night, realm of the 3D ring
Some lauding and praising, others weeping and wailing

UPSIDE-DOWN WORLD

Abuse is their love, drama their peace
Chaos their order, mistreatment their ease
Don't try to understand them, the world of below
An opposite mind, no oneness, just "solo"

"Me" this, "I" that, their eye only egocentric
Delusions of superiority, their pompousness prolific
Stay far away from them or you'll end up disturbed
This is the "freedom" of the unclean caged birds

TARGETING THE WORLD ABOVE

"Let me raise my throne above the stars of El," they echo
The ones from the delusional abyss below
Just as the sun isn't defeated by the darkness of night
The darkness will never depose the Light

But the oppressors still go on oppressing
Their reprobate minds an unstable underpinning
Why won't they stop if they know they've lost?
Well, fools choose folly even if their lives it cost

THE TARES

The tares and the wheat both grew together
Their lives a proving ground for where to spend forever
The latter took it seriously, choosing Yah their Cover
But the tares kept on tearing the whole world over

They suppressed Truth in the choices they made
Mask after mask so their ego wouldn't fade
Choosing flesh and people pleasing all their days
In the mire of their desires, a forever cyclical maze

THE GOATS

Greatest of all time? No, lowest of all divine
No Light inside, drunk with unclean wine
Stubborn and unruly, corrupted within
Their favorite pastime? Chosen sin

Having a form of godliness, a crafted body
Yet rejecting Truth, they remained unholy
We were His witnesses, our eye His camera
Off with them to the lake that burns forev'a

BY THEIR FRUIT

    Pay attention and you'll realize the heart of man
    The energy of his actions a manifested plan,
    Venerating the flesh and the lusts thereof
    Showing he's been cut off from the realms above

    Out of his heart speaks the darkness he chose
    Son of belial, falsehood his prose
    There's no need to be sorry for his lot
    Like you, me and everyone, the same choice he got

THEIR ROOTS

Decoys rooted in the kingdom below
The underworld, an upside-down part of the show
Headquartered in the second heaven, walking in the night
Their pestilence sent into the earth the Truth to fight

Rotten trees, twice dead, plucked up from the roots
Jealousies and strife the darts they shoot
Withered souls embittered by the path they chose
Tricked into the cheap rewards their pride arose

SPIRITUAL LAZINESS

No service never, seeking only pleasure
To be above the Most High their desire
Yahuah takes wondrous care of all creation
These wandering ones only walk in rebellion

"What do you mean we have to put in work?"
The little deviants complain, going berserk
To remain on high is no small task
Yet in glory they still long to bask

VAIN FORM

A form of godliness but denying its power
Covered in dust as lies and darkness devour
Their reaction to the trauma, a result of sin
Fallen state through expulsion from Eden within

"You were in Eden, the garden of Elohim"
Yet rebelled against the order of the shamayim
Coveting power without the work and L.O.V.E.[1] required
And an exalted throne through falsehood desired

---

1. L.O.V.E. - Living in Oneness Vs. Ego

IDOLS

Void of the Holy Spirit while walking the earth
Dolls of destruction since the moment of birth
Ordained to condemnation, going astray from the womb
Empty shells moving around, their bodies a tomb

Cut off from heaven, the kingdom within
They call it "lacking empathy," no true lovin'
Lust is their "love" and a feening for control
Of the mind of another, feasting on their soul

HELL RAISER

The abyss has enlarged itself to welcome them
Hell from beneath rising at their anthem
They ran hastily to death as delusions abounded
By great smoke and dark stench were surrounded

"Trail blazers" these hell raisers called themselves
The wicked one into the pit their souls delves
Once into his snare they were locked perpetually
That's when they realized they'd lost eternally

WICKED PRIZE

They sold their souls to be used by evil
Lower entities, spirits, acting diabolical
For money, status and popularity
They forfeited their inner humanity

Cursed is the one who trusts in man
People pleasing chosen over divine plan
The illusion of the world was their prize
A spiritual blinding darkening their eyes

MORTAL IMMORTALS

They walked the same realm, the tares and the wheat
Until the oppressors' dastardly defeat
All mortals put on immortality
The wheat above, the tares condemned infinity

Chosen ones from sin's bondage released
While oppressors were cut off from the flow of peace
Twisting in the mire of the burning abyss
Darkness and anguish their chosen matrix

CREATURES FROM BENEATH

Crawling out of the depths of the pit
Ghouls, gremlins, imps and hobbits
Disguised in the spectrum of human flesh
Came to ensnare and entrap souls afresh

The minions and legion from the abyss below
Posed as family, friends, people — what a show
In the process of time with Truth as their Beacon
Those from on high learned their necessary lesson

PRIVILEGED DESTRUCTION

Filed on ahead, going forth with their own plan
Pride, pomp and ego spanning entire lifespans
In disrespect and dishonor of Light they remained crude
Unmerited control and entitlement their attitude

This was the way of the serpent and his children
Cycling insanity from generation to generation
The principles from on High, eternal order they bend
Loonie tunes to loonie bin, the pit for all eternity spend

ATTACK OF THE TROLLS

Do you see them? Hidden under suits of flesh
The trolls from beneath the bridge, a miry mess
They never give up do they? The minions of the enemy
Fell once, fell twice, while trespassing earthen territory

Trolls, trolls entering a jurisdiction not their own
Delusional mindset into an empty, devilish void sown
Lamps having gone dim, their hearts painted ebony
Never a vindication, no acquired victory

CROOKED, TWISTED SERPENT

Biting, sucking and draining them dry
The victims uneasy, left wondering why
In darkness they're blinded unable to see
They've entered a union with their soul's enemy

First came doubts and a fear creeping in
Ignorant of its source, themselves they start hating
The entities allowed to roam freely inside
Of the reprobate minds on the other side of the divide

WILD BY NATURE

On the children of the night His wrath abides
The wicked ones who by nature are wild
Covert, manipulative and aggressive, they abuse
Lying without cause while innocents they accuse

Empty idols are these twice dead, rotten trees
Soon brought down on bended knees
Having traded their soul's wealth of true humanity
For meaningless illusion of vain "superiority"

DISTORTED AND DISTURBED

    The loop dee loop of madness
    Never-growing, road of emptiness
    Pride and ego to save, to salvage
    Never mind if turned into a savage

    Mind unstable in all its ways
    Blind, ignorant, left in a daze
    The snare of pleasures robbed them of peace
    Now vain beauty has been turned to beast

TAKEN IN TYRANNY

In flesh of iron and miry clay
These empties they go astray
Their lives an echo of groans of pain
From self-serving ways there was no refrain

In tyrannical madness they rebelled
Choosing only "pleasures" — a self-made hell
Their own choices trapped them in the fray
Soon solar winds come to *take* them away

WICKED TANGO

It's the result of an empty soul, the result of an empty life
They say, "I fill the void;" the void of a life of strife
Repentance needed and a turning back to the Prince of Light
Instead a bed was made in which to die, rendezvous with the Prince of Night

Ignorant and lost in the depth of low consciousness
Attached to a "sense of power," stuck in the realm of emptiness
In a body of death they attack and hurt, an attempt to destroy others
Using pleasure to numb the pain; for them only "power" matters

WICKED TANGO

It's the result of an empty soul, the result of an empty life
They say, "I fill the void;" the void of a life of strife
Repentance needed and a turning back to the Prince of Light
Instead a bed was made in which to die, rendezvous with the Prince of Night

Ignorant and lost in the depth of low consciousness
Attached to a "sense of power," stuck in the realm of emptiness
In a body of death they attack and hurt, an attempt to destroy others
Using pleasure to numb the pain; for them only "power" matters

THE LION

THE LAMB

A TEACHING, A LEARNING

Many enter, walking to and fro
Lessons to teach, a part of the show
Ignorant of this, will they ever know?

From darkness to Light was our destined journey
Back to the Truth of you and me
Once blind but now we see

Mirror within reflecting Truth from the beginning
Lessons learned through reality's springing
Untarnished soul saved by false-self dying

IN THE BEGINNING

    The Word, the Voice of Truth
    Vibration
    Echoing, quickening

    The Spirit of Truth brought Light
    Life
    Birthing, growing

    Refractions of Light over many waters
    Frequencies
    Rising, modulating

THE WORD

The Word, the Voice of the Most High,
Walking in the Garden in the Day
Light fills the mind of man and woman

The Word, the Anointed of Elohim,
Piercing through the darkness
Truth breaks every stronghold of falsehood

The Word, the Son of Yahuah,
Overcoming the world of night
Oneness shatters the eye of pride

IN THE GARDEN

In the Garden, the mind of Truth, a serpent was given a chance
To test the loyalty of Adam whom were given free choice
Would they cling to the Spirit of Truth or believe the spirit of falsehood?

First, fell one and then the other into 3D's false romance
Another eye was opened, the one of the serpent's subtle, strange voice
Onto the chessboard of Day and Night the man and the woman now stood

Generation upon generation, humanity continued the perpetual dance
The Prince of Light then overcame the night, leaving His Word a strong advice
If mankind chose Truth, their hostile mind would be transformed to good

THE LAMB WITHIN

To the Lamb Who set captives free
From the clutches of their enemy
Oh, my Beloved, there is none like Thee

In solitude and rest
You showed what was best
That life is worth living at Your gentle behest

No greater love ever shown
Indeed, none more excellent was ever known
A loving Spirit, Father, King and Prince to call our own

NO GREATER LOVE

As the Voice of Truth enters, L.O.V.E.[1] is close companion
Nothing, yea no one, withstands this qadosh union
He causes those to flee who choose strange rebellion

To seek and to save the lost was His highest mission
Those lost in low consciousness, blinded by lies of man's tradition
Christ spoke the Most High's Words, Keys of eternal life's transformation

Anointed Words of Truth bringing to the knowledge of the Most High
To the ones who did choose misery the repentant soul wondered why
For we inherit the Kingdom within, a deep healing and a joyful cry

---

1. L.O.V.E. - Living in Oneness Vs. Ego

CHRIST IN ME

Everything changed, old man a necessary loss
Putting on divinity
Bearing my cross

The serpent was lifted up, spectrum of flesh
Egocentric mind of darkness
With soul once enmeshed

The old me had to die so I could gain
Oh, eternal Life!
Well worth the pain

GARMENT OF LIGHT

Tongue, power speaking Truth
Ushered in the Spirit
Within pure vessels in whom to inhabit

Harmonious voices of praise
Surrounded with songs of deliverance
A people in reverence of His holy presence

Yah's children put on Light as a garment
Shielded from pit's fall
As He encompasses and fills all

SACRIFICE, WHAT IS?

A chosen humility
Dust used to cover divinity
He became sin, then died for you and me

As the bronze serpent, He was hung upon a tree
Then lifted up, drawing all, an ensign to be
For those desiring to live eternally

Our salvation was bought, it wasn't free
Holy blood was shed on Calvary
We live for Him *now* and in eternity

TRUTH'S BLOOD

"The life of the flesh is in the blood"
Truth's blood has a voice
He speaks, calling from the depths of earth, from heaven

The blood of Truth, of the Word,
Of the Son of Yah Most High, cries out,
"Mercy," while sprinkled on the mercy seat

Abba looks upon the blood of Truth, of His Son
"I shall favour him whom I favour"
He says, "I shall have compassion on him whom I have
    compassion"

THE DOOR

Oh, Good Shepherd of the Way
The pure Lamb
From Whom we'll never stray

Our Bellwether, our eternal Friend
With You from the beginning
Eon upon eon in Thy company to spend

The Door of the sheep, Lover of our soul
None of us lost
Not one the enemy stole

THE BELLWETHER

"Eli, Eli, lamah shebaqtani,"
Mocked and scorned on the hill of Calvary
He became the curse for us, to Him our loyalty

"Cursed is the one who hangs upon a tree"
Our Bellwether's loving sacrifice saved us
None other would we ever trust

"My sheep hear my voice and they follow me"
Indeed we flee from strangers' voices
Wolves in sheep clothing, tempting with vices

L.O.V.E. REQUIRES SPIRIT

True love isn't fitting for a fool
It requires much energy, true power to withstand
The lazy do lazily and none of them understand

In living in Oneness and eschewing ego
The workings of love are shown
Only this Way will He ever be known

Yah indeed chose the "foolish" things to confound the "wise"
And the "weak" to confound the "strong"
Egocentric force loses all day long

---

1. L.O.V.E. - Living in Oneness Vs. Ego

A QUICKENING FLOW

To the pure You show Yourself pure,
Holy, wonderful and kind
In Your love we forever abide

Of this Word we rest assured
From You flow Truth and life
Eternal, unending from pierced side

Most High's Spirit producing fruit galore
Quickened branches of the True Vine
Oh, what L.O.V.E.[1] as deep as is wide!

---

1. L.O.V.E. - Living in Oneness Vs. Ego

OUR GOSHEN

Protected and guarded by life-giving Word
To the right nor to the left
Will we never again turn

No other mighty one, no Word as powerful
None other so True,
Peace-giving and wonderful

Lying tongues, falsehood defeated by the Lamb
As He comes on the clouds of heaven
Executing judgment against the damned

THE LAMB

As bold as the Lion
Of the tribe of Yahudah are the righteous in salvation
Forever in Truth and eschewing the lying, roaring one

Now on the offensive,
Warring in the Word against falsehood oppressive
"Thy kingdom come," is their anthem operative

In them Truth covers the earth as the waters cover the seas,
Baptizing the dysfunctional ones desiring to be made free
Yes, I am in the Lion, and the Lion in me

SHOUT OF THE KING

They run to and fro, madness all about
The still, small Voice has become a shout
Midnight cry, heralding time's out!

Tick tock? No longer
Knock knock, hey stranger
Time to spend eternity with their chosen master

Every knee bow, every tongue confess
Then off to the reward of their own choices
Inherit eternal life or cast out with the lifeless

IDENTITY

Yah is my jewelry
Yah is my crown
He is the praise upon my lips and my renown

I am my Father's, and my Father is mine
To no other do I pertain
From worthless pleasures do I refrain

Onwards and upwards is my journey
The star of my heart shining brighter and brighter
As the Day Star makes His home with me forever

NEVER ALONE

"Lo, I am with you always even to the end of the age"
Words of Life, Words of promise
A balm to the soul in times of distress

Our Prince of peace took the broken pieces
Of you and me and mended the fences
Toward the Most High

Our Lion of the tribe of Yahudah
Reconciled us back to Yahuah
Glory, glory halleluYah!

IN GUARDING I

Over a thousand years
Yet under a century
Knowing I, a lifelong journey

Face of a Lion, cherubim
Guarding the presence of Yah within
I Am Who I Am even still

The beginning is the end
And the end only the beginning
As I learn, I grow in flow of True peace and meaning

SEED IN YAHUAH

I sewed my Seed in Yahuah
And He gave me freedom
Yea

I sewed my Seed in Yahuah
And He gave me the bliss, the bliss
The bliss of all existence

Not caring what the people think
Blue slippers on in the wind
Yea, Freedom flows as Freedom sings

TRIBE

Have you ever seen a people this peculiar?
A tribe invisible
A tribe invincible

Have you ever seen a people of this origin?
A tribe before the beginning
A tribe having no end

Have you ever seen people of this caliber?
A tribe at Oneness
A tribe in Truth

SOLITUDE

Journey taken back to yourself
None other with you but the One within
In the stillness, in the quiet

At times it may be difficult these moments alone
Like uncharted waters, rough waves to pass through
Yet in the silence on your seven seas

An arduous path with an expected end
In the *now* with high hope for the future
Onward and upward through every challenge

REST

In this is confidence
A unending resilience
Life's lessons then, *now* and in the distance

Like the depths of the ocean
Untroubled in every commotion
In Yahuah, love and true devotion

A constant, peaceful flow
What I have, what I know
It is in this freedom I grow, I glow

WELL FED

Eating goodness, eating love
The workings of the Spirit
Of the realms above

Kindness, gentleness, faithfulness too
What will He find
When He checks your fruit?

Name inscribed in the book that gives life
Holy Seed, Holy Tree
None other besides

ALMIGHTY

El Elyon, El Shaddai
Yahuah ben Yahuah
Son of the Most High

Full of Truth
Full of grace
King of kings, none compare to You

True power, rooted in purity
Wiping out falsehood
Heaven on earth, royal mind reality

FOREVER FAVORED

Change this to that
That could be blue, and this could be black
Fully armored against all attack

Thank You, Yah, for Your clarity
Thank You for Your Truth
No more need to hold on to false youth

Left the illusion behind
Detached from the false world
In pure reality has my path, my blessed scroll, unfurled

LOOKING UP

New goals, new vision from the King
Not my will even still
Heaven's Word, His bidding

Love emanating from deep within
Spirit of the great I Am
Truth's wellspring

Lifting mine eyes to the "hill"
Where does my help come from?
The Adon Yahuah in Whom *all* have their being

AT THE ENDING

As it was in the beginning
So it is at the ending
A learning, a teaching

Transitioning to new life, new mind
No looking back, never
Upwards forever

The past forgotten
As the Way forges ahead
Prince of peace leading to the kingdom within

ALL AUTHORITY

All authority
Every moment of victory
Is to the one who is made *one* with the One

To none other our loyalty
To none other our praise
None other so worthy as the King of all kings

The realm where peace abodes
Love, unending joy
And eternal flow

SETTING CAPTIVES

FREE

BORN AND SHAPED

    Once asleep in the dust of the earth
    Ignorant of life's true meaning
    Steeped in darkness since birth
    Clung first to the milk before the weaning

A HOUSE ROBBED

The call comes from inside the house
Deep in its hidden chambers
Obsessive, envious and compulsive
Controlled and overrun by strangers

FALSEHOOD IS A WORLD

The eye at the bottom of the pit
Sends out darkness the whole world over
Ignorant pieces moved across the chessboard
Acting recklessly, then hiding and running for cover

TRUTH IS A KINGDOM

    Light streaming from the worlds above
    Over the depths of this ebony-aired realm
    Beckoning, guiding those seeking Life
    The Spirit of Truth and Wisdom at its helm

BETTER TO BE THAN TO FEEL

Don't come to me to simply *feel* alive
Go to the Source through Jesus Christ
The Word of Truth seated on the throne
To the heavenlies through Him alone

FEELINGS A FLEETING

It's about *being* not focused on feeling
Though feelings will come along with the being
Yet feelings are fleeting much like the wind
Don't know where they come from nor where they're going

NOT THE SAME

They made a deal, ridding their soul of Truth
Abhorring and "selling" the mind superior
They made a deal with the devil for "luxury"
Falling into the mind inferior

DECOY NO LONGER

False jokes and jokers laid aside
External decoy, detected, died
The *real* you, Higher Self, deep inside
By Truth He lives and abides

EMOTIONS

Energy in perpetual motion
Like waves of the ocean
They ebb and flow
Going to and fro

BEING

    Yea, it is better to *be* than to feel
    Inheriting Truth and Freedom's spring
    Making you free from that in which you were lost
    No longer by emotions controlled and tossed

WITHIN THE SOUL

No leaks, bruises nor putrefying sores
But oneness, love and joy galore
Kingdom of Heaven through Christ the only goal
True peace found within the soul

INTERNAL INVINCIBLE ARMY

When the Mind of Christ creates possibility
The Spirit of Yah gifts the ability
To see things through with faith and fidelity
So that resurrected souls inhabit eternity

BREAKING BONDAGE

Words are spirit, false words bring strife
Words are spirit, true words give life
For an imprisoned soul, falsehood brought hell
To set the soul free, the truth we must tell

DECEPTIVE DOMINION

It is the purified one who holds true power
But the counterfeits of dominion by force and falsehood rule
Yet their rulership is temporary until you
See through their illusion and no longer cower

TRAUMA PRINCE

    The prince of darkness who rules through drama
    Abuse, mistreatment and all kinds of trauma
    Was defeated to allow the pure Light in
    Dispelling chaos and ending its cycles within

ON WINGS OF DELIVERANCE

>Balance is vital to the soul's stability
>Harmony to its right agility
>It is for these very reasons
>Deliverance is crucial in its season

PRINCE OF PEACE

    Prince of Peace, Who is Truth and Light
    Christ Yeshua pierced through the darkness of night
    Brought balm to the soul of the prisoner
    Revealing the Most High's true glorious nature

TRUTH, LOVE, JUSTICE

Oh, ye principles of pure, higher mind
Through works of righteousness your jewels we find
The kingdom enlightened from journeys inside
Under your wings do we forever abide

THEY SAY TRUTH HURTS

When we to delusions cling
Truth become excruciating
But if we let go, hold to vanity no more
Then the wellspring of healing we ensure

OUR ROCK

A sure place and solid footing
To none other is our trusting
Our El Elyon, Yahuah El Shaddai
Eloah Almighty, our Abba Most High

A HOUSE BUILT

A house built without human hand
Is the one redeemed in this lifespan
Whose spirit has been made alive
From the depths newly revived

HICCUP

The one doing right falls, but gets back up again
"Never give up" is their anthem
Not to be caught up in dysfunctional ways
From the snare of bondage is their sure escape

WHY PAIN?

In this realm of duality exist pain and pleasure
The lazier you are, the more you suffer
The more ignorant you are, the more you consume
Multiplying the pleasure and the pain too

PURPOSE IS POWER

Have you lived a meaningless life?
At times in misery looking for light
When purpose is found it *is* true treasure
A reason to be besides seeking for pleasure

MESSENGERS MULTIPLIED

Oh, Messengers, clean spirits ministering
Burning lamps, fellow light beings
Sent to strengthen those who choose life
Gathering them unto new world on high

LIGHT

    Yahuah makes His face to shine
    Oh, Word, Light divine
    You awake the dawn
    Oh, bright, Morning Star!

PAIN, PURPOSE, POWER

Pain comes at emerging Light's revelation
Purpose flows forth ending delusion
Power enables strengthening Truth's reality
In that order we move and walk in destiny

A SURE WORD

Word of warfare, Word of Truth
Setting us free from all falsehood
Deceitfulness of riches holds no sway
Over the heart enlightened by the Way

ENEMIES EXPELLED

    Howling, growling, menaces to life
    Enemies expelled yet putting up a fight
    They found no place in transformed vessel
    New world, new mind, rid of evil

THE GREAT CALM

"Rest, enter into My rest"
Kingdom of heaven's call
The call from within the soul
Of the one in great calm

CAPTIVES MADE FREE

All prisoners have been set free
Those who answered, "Follow Me"
Out of the dark cave they were called
Into the Light of the glorious Son

NO
LONGER
CONDEMNED

NEW CREATURE

Made a new creature out of the two
The seed of the serpent no longer an issue
His head crushed, and the soul healed indefinitely
The enmity for all time abolished completely
Once was opaque, a body of shame
Now transparent and without blame
Conscience not seared with a hot iron
For Truth was chosen as our Beacon
Fleshly mind crucified with its cyclical moods
The highest frequency is our mind renewed

Reconciled to Yahuah

ETERNITY *NOW*

    Infinity in cycles again and again
    Round and round viciously, without an end
    Chaos and drama, existing in misery
    Clinging to the crowd, fleshly company
    Until the pathway of Light was revealed
    Of healing, of rest and true loving received
    Eternity in growth eon upon eon
    New, higher heights above and beyond
    Peace and a great calm, living in oneness
    Clinging to Truth and the great clouds of witness

    In the eternal Kingdom not of this world

THE CROSSINGS

At the crossings, the realm of day and night
A mixture of worlds, parts with and without light
A chance to make a choice, live or die
Follow the Truth or exist in the lie
The bladder of the fish, the checkerboard
World stage with its curtains widely scattered
In every moment, a choice, an action
A choice to grow in Day or in darkness to be stationed
When choosing Light, the Way to freedom
Truth gives liberty and the right to overcome

Fully crossed over into Life

NOT CONDEMNED

"Neither do I condemn you," says He
The One to whom I owe loyalty
To live a life for Him alone
After such sweet sacrifice shown
Discipline, dedication, determination too
My path cleared, a destiny in Truth
Old ways forgotten, past life wiped clean
Mentally and spiritually better than I've ever been
All things are possible as I walk in true freedom
No limitations in this peaceful, abundant kingdom

New life in Christ

AUTONOMY

Resist the enemy and he will flee
Walking in the Word and humility is the key
Spiritual fortitude found in the Most High
No other sovereign to whom I cry
My only Guide, Company and Friend
Forever with me, even until the end
Others carry titles whom many laud and observe
Yet there is only One Whom I wish to please and serve
Who gives me autonomy and encourages me
To guard His Word as He promises sure victory

Not unto us, but unto Your Name give glory

PERCEPTION

Mind's eye, mind's eye, oh, eye of the mind
What did you capture? Yea, what did you bind?
"Write the vision and make it plane upon tablets"
Inscribe it on the heart of man before he forgets
The Way to life eternal, the Truth in the soul
Vital to life and the path he should go
Was once in dysfunction, manifesting mingled mess
Until Light entered, and he was turned from darkness
His chaos forgiven and his day brighter be
Finally whole through a determined will to truly see

Eye single, body full of Light

A NEW WORLD

What has happened over night?
Like a dream the past is out of sight
It's other worldly for in the twinkle of an eye
The Most High answered our distressed cry
All the world may have been just a stage
But renewed are we for the coming age
Once was darkness and now we're light
Our soul was saved through His might
A beautiful life does He reveal
Manifested beyond the old reel

The veil was torn

MINDSET IS VITAL

The mind holds within it a perceiving lens
Interpreting the world through every sense
Its perceptions were oftentimes faulty
Deeming this and that unworthy
While overvaluing that which profited nothing
Causing much loss of life's true meaning
An electric shock shattered that false veil
Rendering the system an obvious fail
Christ restored balance and harmony once more
And the soul ceased from suffering sore

A necessary and life-changing shift of mind

PRICKED PRIDE

Pride was the lodestone of every scar
Keeping the heart bound in a jar
Its only escape was the crushing of that stone
But the heart was incapable of acting on its own
Imprisoned with no way out was its strong belief
No one was thought able to offer true relief
Until Christ, the Life, the Truth and the Way
Offered hope, peace, joy, increased faith and a brighter day
He pulverized the lodestone with the soul's thirst for Truth
Holy Spirit fire creating transparent crystal, made new

Humility, the sacrifice of a broken and contrite heart

THE MIRACLE OF TEARS

Salt of earth mingled with water
Droplets infused with healing power
Pouring, releasing, an effective refreshing
Moments of meeting the Great Physician within
Miraculous Medicine emanating from inside
By Him we live, move and abide
Wellspring of the rivers of the water of life
Truth bubbling like a geyser rising high
The stream then appears, dampening the cheek
Moments of healing, proving effective for the meek

For the spiritual health of the soul

A TRIGGERING

"What has happened here?"
The soul cried out in fear
At the time it hadn't seemed too serious
But the crushing within grew grievous
The world suddenly painted blue
A loss of "solid" stance in you
The threshold, the point of no return
Was breached as boundaries within were burned
Soul's safeguards, the unsteady walls
Creaked and swayed crashing beneath it all

The darkness before the dawn

BALM FOR THE SOUL

Though you never asked to be lied to
It happened when the world got a hold of you
Inhumane machine churning out deceptive "desires"
While consuming parts of the soul it pretended to admire
The beast became arrogant and usurped its position
On borrowed time it was and increased in diabolical sedition
The Anointed's unfolding plan was the saving of the soul
Reinstating the Word of Truth and returning Him to His rightful role
As the ruling Spirit and steady foundation within
You were never overcome by the wily beast ever again

Our Redeemer, our Helper, our Friend

CROWN "JEWELS"

They placed fiction as truth and Truth as fiction
Mortal words fail to fully relate their devious actions
Many living souls, witnesses perceiving it all
While still others blind, unaware through the fall
Crowns, scepters and orbs with jewels filled
Channeling energies that deceivers never held within
Their dominion false, of the external "natural" world
An illusion in the mind of the spiritually unlearned
If you desire Truth it will set you free
Of the delusion that true power lies outside of thee

They need jewels (crystals, precious stones); you are in the Anointed One

HOUSES: FROM SAND TO ROCK

Houses made with hands can never satisfy
The souls stranded in a land that's salty and dry
No water in sight, nothing to reassure the marooned
Those who made their beds on hardened sand dunes
Their landlord loved it so, for he had a scheme in store
To make of them fish bait on his simulated seashore
Little did he know that through the process of time
They'd choose Truth, discovering his falsehood and lies
Michael stood up and said, "It is done!"
Houses saved by the Rock, the victory won

You are His house, His temple made without hands

CONVERTED

Now up from what was once down
Death is gone as new life is crowned
Those who were lost were finally found
No more to destruction were they bound
Their mind transformed from night to Day
On solid ground and from its path they do not stray
Called, chosen and forever faithful
Having been changed, they remain eternally grateful
Living out their days in abundance and peace
From sin's chains have they been released

A converted heart brought life and peace

HELD FAST

Earth's many cruel ones boasted that they were skilled
But didn't have the power to break what they didn't build
The power of earth's chosen ones is from the Most High
In His secret place do they forever reside
Not easily provoked, they perceived when wickedness
Came bulldozing in, attempting to make a mess
They kept the faith while watching for the enemy
As the cruel ones, in a rage, strove to make away many
The chosen held fast to the Word of the Way
Forever guarding the Truth come what may

In times of adversity, stand firm and see Yah's deliverance

FORTIFIED CITY

We have chosen peace and will not rely
On anything or anyone other than the Most High
After many trials, tests and tribulations
We remain loyal to Truth over desire of nations
We fought the good fight and finished the race
And now abide within Yahuah's embrace
His wall of fire wraps around us as a shield
To a doubting lower mind will we never again yield
Prepared and perfected in Elohim's refined armor
His Word on our tongue, bringing healing and ardor

We remained in ordained position, having done all to stand

FROM WEB TO WAY

World's eyes
Web of lies
Along came the spider

Full of tricks
We panicked
But there was One wiser

Truth was told
His Way behold
Salvation for our souls, the Provider

Soon enough, the dragon crushed

In Truth now and ever

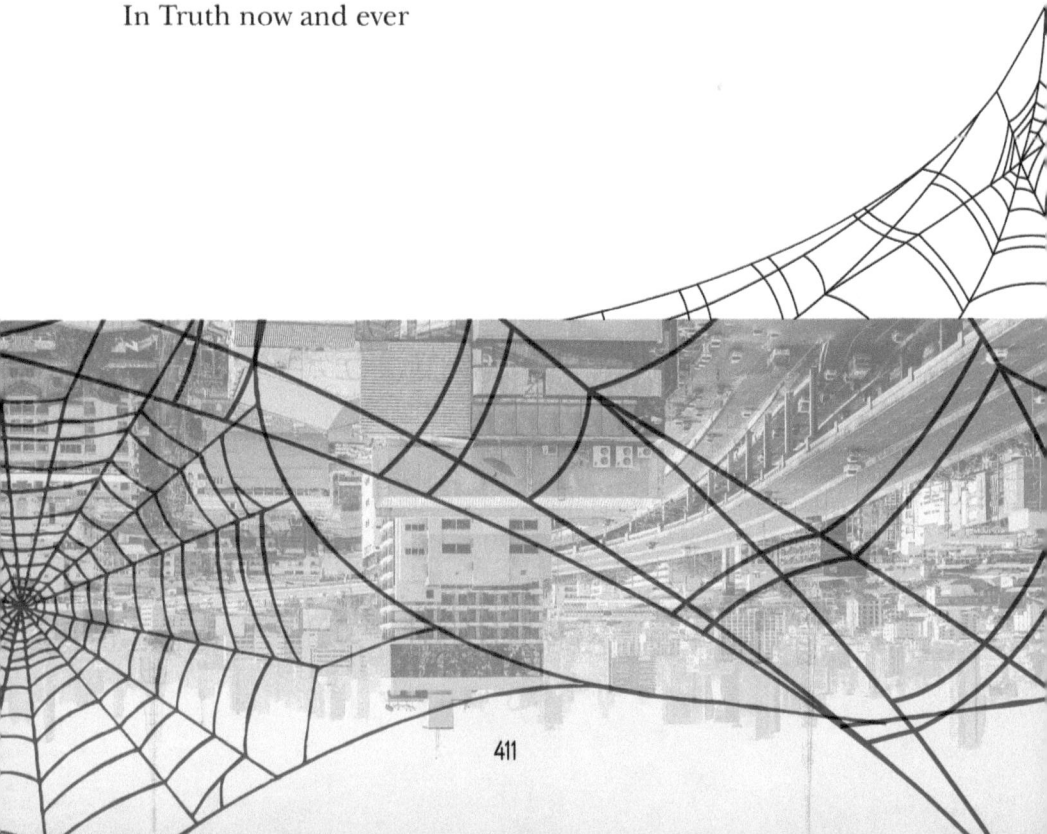

BREAKTHROUGH

The bulb broke, its energy not sedentary
But ascending to new form and new territory
This was not a physical place
'Twas high, another space
A new timeline altogether
Selfish pride and ambition thrown under
Of service to Truth the only role
Pleasing the Most High the will's goal
Mind and emotions, though under attack
Determined to fight, for there was no turning back

"Endure to the end!" is the loud cry

COURAGE

"Do not be afraid," He said, seeing
That fear impedes peace flowing
"Be strong and courageous," He commanded
As opposers of our souls our life demanded
We boasted only in knowing and understanding
Abba Yahuah, our Eloah and King
This strength and courage emanates from the Word
When righteousness and Truth are done and heard
The power to will and to forever do
What is right and pleasing in the eyes of You

We trust *only* in Yahuah Sabaoth

REVEALED

What the carbuncle meant to obscure was made clear
The sudden gift of enlightenment, the Word did steer
Upward and higher unto the Truth that makes free
Didn't know you were drowning until you finally breathed
Air for the first time filling your lungs
As your legs o'er yonder bridge hung
Still wet from the depths you moved away from the fright
Clinging fiercely to life in a new realm, a new height
In the solitude of a world outside of time
Rest was afforded, a peace sublime

After the revelation, peace

RESISTANCE

Witchcraft, rebellion, word curses and sorcery
Yet as an angel of light doth appear the enemy
Attacks aplenty, so be on guard to know when
His wiles, his tactics, as he sends his children
Their reward, their boon, their ultimate goal
Their greatest delight is in destroying your soul
Having this knowledge of the way they move
Be sober, be vigilant and never thyself lose
Resist the devils, and they will always flee
And you'll be freed from the snare of the enemy

First, the attack; then, the victory in Christ followed by strengthening

EMANATIONS

Started out thinking you were not enough
In a world advertising the need for more stuff
The time spent in darkness wrested control
Another held a force that blinded your soul
At the gentle beckoning of the Word, your will
Opened your heart and allowed the Self within
The one who is one with the One inside
Who emanated true words, bringing forth life
That quickening surge and its flowing power
Cleared your vision from that same hour

Your whole body will be full of Light

ONE VOICE

Like a steady rock resting on deep seafloor
Is the one who desires to chase no more
The oohs and ahhs of the ever-growing crowd
No matter how tempting, no matter how loud
Many speaking all around
Yet one voice inside be found
Moments in quietness and peace
Journeys within revelations release
Treasures of life flowing in the calm
Spirit of Truth unending awakes the dawn

Voice of freedom, voice of rest

ETERNAL FAMILY

Our only family are those who do Your will
No matter the sacrifice of the old life's thrills
As challenging the lessons of life we must learn
From Your Word, Your Way, we wish not to turn
Already wed to your Holy Spirit of Truth
Committed to none other but You
A discerning eye and a mind on You stayed
Try as they might we will not be swayed
We've seen past the falsehood and vanity of things
We know from where true hope and life springs

The eternal family of Truth, Way, Life

RIPPLES

A large stone thrown into the deep
Makes a difference for those who sleep
In the darkness, the black of night
Though seemingly calm, there is no light
Many can't see below the surface
But they watch the ripples and can only guess
The damage done by that large one
As it sunk below the horizon
If those ripples were to be believed
Many a soul would be made to grieve

It takes just one to affect the many

WATCH AND PRAY (JAMAICAN PATOIS)

Watch out fi di roaring lion
Cause 'im a roar, 'im a come
'Im a look fi victim
Mi seh 'im a roar, 'im a come
'Im a look fi victim
Shield inna u left, Sword inna u right han
Ready your stance, you're no longer the damned
Mi seh tell di people dem
Watch out fi di roaring lion
Cause 'im a roar, 'im a come

'Im a look fi victim

A GLORIOUS VICTORY

LIFE ETERNAL

This is heaven, this is bliss
I'm in heaven and nothing's amiss

One with the Father and the family of Yah
Yeshua, Jesus, the Way, I Am in awe

Holy Spirit of Truth my Comforter
True, divine nature my only Cover

The altogether, all encompassing Light
Turning to full Day what was once partially night

No longer ashamed nor walking in the flesh
My mind transformed, new life afresh

TRUE POWER

They couldn't steal our humanity
But were still a necessary part of the story
Their force through their shame and vanity
Mockers and imitators wanting to steal glory

They were ignored as we trained our focus on Yah Most High
Old self, the infernal ego, died the death long ago
As the One pointed us to Heaven, the Higher "I"
So that we would live and His true glory show

Our power was in knowledge of our true identity
Knowing where we came from and where we were going
To the heavenly Zion on high, Yah's Holy City
Through the gates would He His people bring

THE LAMB'S WIFE

To the Bridegroom we say, "It was worth the wait"
Though difficult was the way and narrow was the gate
We finished the long journey on our path to freedom
And became forever a wife of an eternal kingdom

HEEL OF POWER

A body was given, shaped in the heart of earth
Moulded in the matrix, a hidden network
By generous miracle the canal was exited in safety
But a dragon was waiting with tools of cruelty

Beneath the stealth and guise of a health check
He bit into the heel this subtle suspect
Blood collected there for nefarious purposes
Fulfilling the first part of the prophecy of Genesis

Before the age of a couple months old
That babe was already fighting against the bold
A dastardly enemy forming mischief by law
Already with many a newborn waging war

To the end of attempting to prevent the crushing
His head already paranoid of the Word manifesting
Yet no amount of masking and deceitful acts
Could hold back the Most High's counter attacks

That babe grew to a ripened age
Coming to the Truth that the whole world's a stage
After the initial bruise to the heel was the journey to healing
New life breathed by the Holy Spirit's revealing

The inevitable fulfillment of the Word of the Most High
A dragon couldn't prevent from coming nigh
Its head worried sick, yoked with madness
Desperate to prevent what it knew would be loss

The heel came down and crushed its head
Casting it out into its infinite sick bed
The hellish pit of its own chaotic choosing
Which rose up to meet him at his coming

All the dragon's hosts who'd done his bidding
Who were in sheep's clothing, in light masquerading
Were buried with him in the world beneath the crossing
A realm of only darkness, fighting, chaos and suffering

That mighty heel was powered by the Spirit of Truth
The Word by Whom the set apart ones were rescued
Carried on high into the Kingdom of Light
A realm of only goodness, a realm with no night

BYGONES

No more sorrow, nor crying, nor tears
One, four, four — all of them sealed
Singing the new song of the lamb
As they took the final stand

The former things now passed and gone
No memory of them any more
Leaves of the tree dressed for their healing
Of a time ago of which was wiped all feeling

New realm, new state of elevation
Was the reward of consecration
Glorification in new world, new eye
Is our lovely, sweet by and by

SONS OF LIGHT

Children of the Day
You, sons of Light
You overcame
Yea, you won the fight

Though you didn't start the war
Rising to the call, you finished in the Son
Never would the Night overcome the Day
Just as the moon can't outshine the sun

Children of the Day
You, Light's sons
You overcame
Yea, the war you've won!

A PLACE CALLED PEACE

Peace is a place, an eternal keep
A pathway to where many do not go
Yet at the appointed time
Few seek for it

Peace is a Spirit, an eternal One
The Way to Whom many do not find
But at the appointed time
Chosen ones find Him

Peace is a mind, a safeguarded world
A state to which many do not reach
Still at the appointed time
Some choose it

SERENITY

Savior, the Word, rooted within
Ever quickening and deep loving
Rivers of the water of life released
Eternity in Truth, love and peace
Newly transformed, all clearly seen
Infinite thanks and praises be
To the One Who is true, loving and kind
Yahuah our Abba, Eloah Most High

LOVE-KISSED

Living in peace
Living in wisdom
Living in oneness
In the eternal kingdom

My Beloved returned
And kissed me sound
Breathing new life in the one
Who was once lost, but now is found

Love-kissed
I've been love-kissed
Living in oneness, I've been love-kissed

Living in peace
Living in wisdom
Living in oneness
In the eternal kingdom

REIGN ETERNAL

Power to lay life down
Power to take it back up again
The command of the Most High to His children

Christ holds the keys of hell and of death
Death could not keep us jailed
Neither could the gates of hell against us prevail

The Word gave us the keys to Life
We hold to and keep the Truth
The eternal reign in the kingdom too

CONSUMING FIRE

How can Consuming Fire be so loving?
Kind, compassionate and compelling
Spirit so pure, full of character
To You only is our soul's desire

Walking in Truth
With the Consuming Fire
Surrounded by burnings
Yet not destroyed

Living in the Light of Him
Loving Him, guarding Him
Lauding Him, serving Him
How can Consuming Fire be so loving?

FINE BRASS

Refined in the furnace
Tried seven times
Purified and made white

Garments a-glowing
Peace a-flowing
Resting well in the Father of Lights

Dwelling with the Consuming Fire
On His holy mount
Fine brass, fine brass, shining only for the Most High

WHITE LINEN

Obscurity to transparency
Unclean to pure
Darkness to light
Eternal life ensured

Filthy rags to white linen
Unstable to newly gifted stone
Brokenness to wholeness
Lost, now found, never alone

EYE SALVE

I asked for eye salve, and my eye was anointed
I bought gold tried in the furnace, and I was made rich
I needed white raiment, and my shame was covered
This is the power of Christ, my Savior

Working from the true kingdom within
The Spirit of Truth moved about transforming
My chaos was changed to resonant peace
From programmed bondage I was released

CROWNS

The still, small Voice beckoned as we drew near
No longer in bondage nor burdened by fear
Crowns of life, the Word He breathed
Onto which we held fast and above all esteemed

We regarded none higher for none loved us so
Not one could ever even come close
Remaining loyal to Him our only desire
An eternal loving for He is our treasure

It happened within, a coronation without hands
Eternal life given for many lifespans
With Him we were before this world was
And we'll forever love Him as He first loved us

LIVING CRYSTAL

Water from His throne like crystal
The firmament between the waters too
From Abba Yahuah do these both issue

From the pineal into the life of the creature
Temples made without hands, His dwelling
Inside the crystalline structure found within

Meditate on this Word and *see* things **through**
Brain sand, these crystals, His throne
The waters above divided from the waters below

Walk by the Holy Spirit and not by the flesh
Portals will open as the Kingdom of heaven comes
You will find yourself supping with Spirit, Father and Son

SAPPHIRE STONE

His throne like a sapphire stone
On the other side of the azure blue
Firmament was above, see there now below
Bow of promise an emerald green
As we walk upon the glassy sea
Living in a purer lens with which we now see
New fruit to taste every month
On this and that side of the river
Waters of life, of Truth do flow
Moving with the Consuming Fire

THRONE ROOM

Only the trustworthy who've proven themselves such
Those who've been responsible with little and with much
Are gifted the right to enter in and sit down
Inheriting a throne, a scepter and an eternal crown

FOUNDATION

Twelve pearls, twelve stones
Pillars built up of living souls
Comprising the temple of the One we love
Now and forevermore

The city's foundation lies foursquare
Light from the Son within doth appear
No need of a sun nor of a moon
Now and forevermore

Twelve foundations, twelve gates
At its core the Lamb awaits
Communion with Whom is our portion
Now and forevermore

LIVING STONES

Living stones, foundations stones
Spiritual house built up for His presence
Urim, thummim, He's pleased with our service
White stone given to those granted acceptance

Living Stone cut out without human hand
Rejected Stone became the head of the corner
Smote the kingdoms and destroyed their plans
It was Yah's doing to bring Him every honor

Living stones, fiery stones of Eden
In Mount Zion, Truth's eternal well
A name written within which no one else knows
Inhabiting the heavenlies where peace dwells

KINGDOM

>King of kings is He
>Lord of lords, the One in me
>*His* glory you see

AN APPOINTED TIME

What is the victory, and what was the war?
The soul held fast in every hour
Even throughout the impossible times
When attacked without reason or rhyme

We overcame by the Lamb's precious blood
And by the Word of our testimony we withstood
The lies and delusion of the world
As the enemy's plan unfurled

At a certain hour, we were brought forth
As witnesses of heaven's high courts
Lessons were learned, challenges overcome
And at the appointed time, the victory we won

CRESCENDO

Oh, my soul gives thanks to You, Abba
Oh, how my soul rejoices in You, Yahuah
My sure Home, my eternal Trust
Making my boast in You a must

Everything else has faded away
For You are my Home and my Stay
You keep me in perfect peace
Growing in love, and joy's release

Wiping away my every tear
To make them no longer near
Leaves of the trees of the garden within
From which I glean my forever healing

FULL THROTTLE

You have come with Your ten thousands
To render judgement and recompense
You will deliver just reward to the hosts of bondage
Those who destroyed Truth and chose only concupiscence

The Word from Your mouth, a two-edged sword
As You speak the sound of many waters
Falsehood is laid waste, to the ground hurled
The scale is balanced where justice matters

"It is finished," the Holy One said
Heavenly sentence meted out for all time
What the cruel have done has fallen upon their own heads
As Yah's people return to their position in the Land Divine

THE FULNESS OF VICTORY

Overcoming the evil with the good
Once confused but now understood
When provoked to anger, and with frustrations filled
Remember His command, "Peace. Be still"

Truth, peace and serenity are the goal
As the momentary waves wash over your soul
Though stones are thrown into the depth of calmness
An unperturbed soul never relinquishes its rest

This is the fullness, the undeterred victory
That those called and chosen have as their testimony
They loved the Most High until the very end
Within His sweet rest do they eternities spend

AN ETERNAL REJOICING

Dark world with a structure of limits
But the brethren escaped that lower eye
They saw outside of that visible spectrum
Thanks to the Word of the Most High

The crossing was slowly discovered
Its outer bands of electromagnetic waves
A sort of chessboard with its pieces
The world stage on hidden display

At the time of harvest
The wheat was gathered in
Their brethren delivered
Heaven excelled in rejoicing

FAMILY OF **ONE**

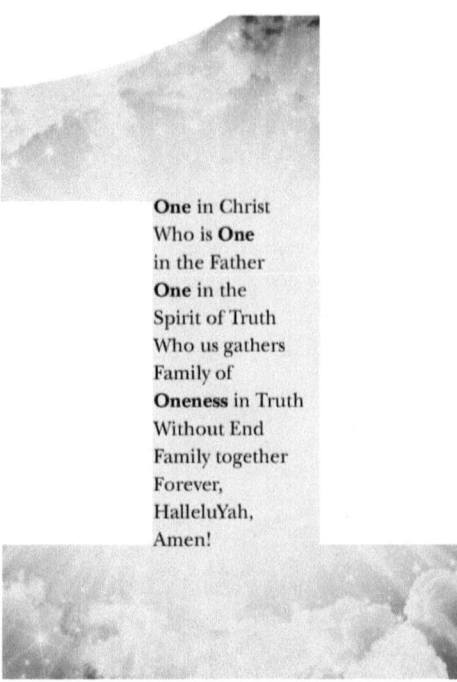

One in Christ
Who is **One**
in the Father
One in the
Spirit of Truth
Who us gathers
Family of
Oneness in Truth
Without End
Family together
Forever,
HalleluYah,
Amen!

Oneness in Truth Without End
So be it. So let it be ...

ACKNOWLEDGMENTS

The lessons that have been granted to me by Yahuah Elohim, that I've had to learn though at times challenging and intense, through experiences with relatives, friends, associates, coworkers and many others. Those enlightening and revelatory moments extended well beyond their scope and were instrumental in the healing and remembrance process that was the creation of this book.

I would be remiss if I did not mention those who resisted my presence, who held me in contempt or who attempted to thwart my growth and elevation in the Holy Spirit of Truth for their own reasons (whatever they may be). I love you. You were indelible stepping stones to victory, and I wish you growth. My hope is that a desire for Truth is birthed within you sooner rather than later .

ABOUT THE AUTHOR

Sasha-Marie Marshall is an avid reader, researcher and truth seeker. Her Works are written with the intention to inspire, as catalysts for change and introspection. She hopes that those who read and perceive the Word come away with a deeper level of self-awareness and a desire for restoration and growth toward Oneness in Truth.

Her advice to all is to live their purpose by aligning themself with the Creator of the Kingdom within, in the name of Yeshua Ha'Mashiach, Jesus Christ, the Word of Truth.

Visit her website at sashamariemarshall.com.